D1546905

THERE ARE THINGS
WE LIVE AMONG

JENNIFER

MOXLEY

FLOOD EDITIONS CHICAGO

THERE ARE THINGS WE LIVE AMONG

ESSAYS ON THE OBJECT WORLD

Published by Flood Editions

www.floodeditions.com

ISBN 978-0-9838893-2-8

Design and composition by Quemadura

Printed on acid-free, recycled paper

in the United States of America

This book was made possible in part

through a grant from the Illinois Arts Council

Earlier versions of some of these essays

appeared in the print journal *Verse*

and in the online journal *Markszine*

First Edition

FOR DIANA, WHO TOOK ME

TO THE PAPER MOON

The greatest poverty is not to live
In a physical world, to feel that one's desire
Is too difficult to tell from despair . . .

WALLACE STEVENS

PREFACE

I conceived of this book while translating *Sleep's Powers*, a collection of essays on sleep by the French poet Jacqueline Risset. Working on that project was delightful. Risset's essays were relatively short, from a few paragraphs to three or four pages long. True essays, in the tradition of Montaigne, they drew on personal experience, literary example, and philosophical question. She included no citations or notes. She explored her topic in ways both provocative and thoughtful, yet free of didacticism or righteousness. The longer I worked on my translation, the more I couldn't help writing (in my head) my own set of corresponding essays on sleep, or thinking of "sleep examples" that Risset had neglected to include. The essay, in her hands, like the best of conversations, awakened my own experiences with and around sleep and gave me new egress into the possible meanings of a subject I had never before thought much about. When the work was finished, I knew I wanted to try my hand at the form.

But I knew I couldn't write about sleep, as it isn't a central passion of mine. For several months I tossed around other ideas. I thought of writing about memory, but dismissed it as too grand. I thought of writing about privacy, but thought it too political. I cannot recall the moment when the "object world" presented itself as my topic, but when it did, I intuitively knew it to be right. I *do* have a passion for things, I thought, long-standing, motivating, and fervent. I remember much of my childhood as emotionally shaped by my imaginative projection onto objects, which served as company as well as vectors for fantastical narratives. In a young adulthood marked by grief through the successive loss of both parents and a dear friend, objects became keepers of the lost life, what I could hold onto. I tried to express this new dimension of things—in this case those that had belonged to my mother —in my poem "Behind the Orbits":

> I checked the house before I left for fragments
> of forgotten consequence, a piano
> remained, a Windsor chair, a fold-down desk
> with a broken hinge whose cubbies had been
> thoughtlessly filled with: paper clips, pencils,

> dry stamps and black coins, mechanical rig
> for a manual mind to scratch near dry
> a waterless leaf. Time was not trapped in
> these things as I, who had loved their user,
> would be . . .

As soon as I had my topic I had my title, knowing that I would write about George Oppen's poem "Of Being Numerous." I have always loved the way the opening lines, "There are things / We live among 'and to see them / Is to know ourselves,'" connect "things" to both self-knowledge and structural assumptions. Oppen's poem provided me a template for writing about how things define us, as well as about the politics of things, and how they function in literature and philosophy. He helped me to explore the paradox of living in a materialistic culture that yet exalts idealist philosophical and religious traditions.

As the work on my book of essays progressed, the apparent limitlessness of the object world, though strangely comforting, began to narrow. I was freed of the worry that I might exhaust my topic, as well as of the need to be inclusive. Jeffrey Robinson, in introducing his book of essays on Romanticism, *The Walk*, puts it this way: "Though

I range through the truly vast and ever-expanding literature of walking, I have eschewed as a goal the frightening lure of comprehensiveness. No one has ever engaged me on the subject of walking literature who has not offered an instance that 'simply can't be left out.'" Just as Risset's omissions had the effect of building sleep narratives in my mind, the mere mention of Robinson's topic provoked examples and excitement in others. What you *leave out,* therefore, is a gift. It is as quintessential to the essay as what you put in. To suggest, and then move on. To set the table for talk, propose a topic, and then spare your interlocutors your comprehensive thoughts. As Mallarmé put it, "it is not *description* which can unveil the efficacy and beauty of monuments . . . but rather *evocation, allusion, suggestion.*" The pleasure of the essay comes from *not* getting to the "bottom of things," but instead letting them stay, in some measure, unknown and mysterious, touched only by a passing thought, evanescent, and easily changeable.

THERE ARE THINGS
WE LIVE AMONG

THE MINERAL FACT

> There are things
> We live among 'and to see them
> Is to know ourselves.'

Not an epigraph, but an opening: to George Oppen's long poem "Of Being Numerous," as well as to my book. When a young poet I read these lines literally, as a more personal version of Williams Carlos Williams's "no ideas but in things." They were a direct statement of fact with which I agreed. I did not take note of the scare quotes, which may indeed have been Oppen's way of qualifying the sentiment. And yet, I knew that the "things" he spoke of were not abstract. They were real material objects, otherwise how could we see them?

Influenced by poets much invested in the "materiality of language," I made "Of Being Numerous" a thing that reflected back my concerns. I read it as a meditation on the "shipwreck of the singular," as a utopian Marxist essay about the difficulty of building community in a world of commerce—of things—and a record of isolation caused by the capitalist system. I heard Oppen's tone as existentially pleading and run through with sadness: a reflection of my youthful preoccupations.

"Crusoe // We say was / 'Rescued.' / So we have chosen." I loved these lines in particular. I was drawn to their cadence, and to the concept of agency made implicit by the word "chosen." But now I wonder, what is Oppen really saying here? Why is the word "rescued," like those words in the opening of the poem, in scare quotes? Did Crusoe's rescue shipwreck him anew? Would he have been better off dead than returned to the state "of being numerous"? Perhaps Crusoe could only know himself when he lived alone with his things. Given that, what does it mean to be numerous? To be denied the ownership of one's things? (A capitalist's fear of communism).

But the diction of the poem's opening is precise: we do not "own" things, we "live among" them. We are separate from the world of objects, though our identity is reliant upon it. By using the word "ourselves" instead of "one's self," Oppen honors his title and the experience of being one among many. Yet the poem will go on to defend the individual and the specificity of each person against the anonymous crowd. A lifelong Marxist, Oppen understood the necessity as well as the risk "of being numerous." As he writes, "Of lives, single lives / And we know that lives / Are single." Honoring our singularity, Oppen proceeds to seal off the world: "As the world, if it is matter, / Is impenetrable." Against it, despite what he calls "the pure joy / Of the mineral fact," each of us will fail: "The power of the mind, the / Power and weight / Of the mind which / Is not enough, it is nothing / And does nothing // Against the natural world."

The poem's paradoxes compel me to delve into that mysterious preposition *of*—so key to conjuring the ambiguity of Oppen's title. According to one dictionary, "of" expresses "the relationship between a part and a whole." Between the individual and the collective, or the single and the many. Consulting another source, I read that "of ... had already developed in Anglo-Saxon various uses involving the idea of *moving* or *resulting from*." In this definition the "shipwreck of the singular" becomes a *result* "of being numerous." The nameless, faceless city, Oppen's language of New York. I am reminded of the nineteenth-century poet's fear of anonymity, of being swallowed up by the city and by modernity. Poe's "The Man of the Crowd" and Baudelaire's "Les Sept Vieillards" *qui se multipliait.*

It is true, "Of Being Numerous" *is* an urban poem. Yet the things within it that help us to know ourselves are not the cold architectural achievements of modernism, "A city of the corporations // Glassed / In dreams" (like the disorienting reflections of Jacques Tati's *Playtime* maze), or the threatening helicopter overhead, "The fly in the bottle," but rather those things that become more meaningful with use. Old apartments, the brick "The eye picks" that was set in place before we were born. One finds a living signature of past lives imbedded in old things. This explains why the great stone pylon etched "1875" leads to a definition of consciousness. It is something "Which has nothing to gain, which awaits nothing, / Which loves itself." It may have nothing to gain, in the sense of *advancement,* but without the traces of past lives around it—old things—how shall it know itself? The existence of things, taken in toto, is indeed an "unmanageable pantheon"; but taken piecemeal, one thing at a time, it transforms into a living, human story, a story, according to Oppen's poem, of "such solitude as we know," and of the melancholia inherent in the mineral fact of being, ending in a hospital bed, with a generic "nurse" being "the last / Who will see him / Or touch him."

One final etymological tributary: "of: indicating the material, substance, parts, or elements composing or used in making anything." What are we made out of? Of things? To believe so confirms the labor theory of value, that is to say, the idea that a thing's value can only be measured by the amount of human labor that went into its production. Or is it rather that *our* value is constituted by the number of things we make? In either case we must glorify things to glorify the labor that goes into making them. If we devalue the things, we devalue the labor. But what if those whose labor produced the things cannot live among them? If we are denied access to the things we make, how shall we know ourselves? Rehearsing this question, I run an errand. I see on the car ahead of me a bumper sticker that reads, "The Best Things in Life Aren't Things." Having just begun writing a book about things, I feel perturbed by this flippant truism. Is a life of *making* worth nothing? Which leads me to start thinking about the economy of poetry . . .

After Robinson Crusoe washes up on his "Island of De-spair," the meagerness of his possessions drives him into a temporary madness: "I had nothing about me but a knife, a tobacco-pipe, and a little tobacco in a box; this was all my provision, and this threw me into such terrible agonies of mind that for a while I ran about like a mad-man." The loss of his companions is of secondary con-cern.

Later he is much comforted by his luck at recovering many more things from the ship: gunpowder, spirits, and tools:

> Then it occurred to me again how well I was furnished for my subsistence, and what would have been my case if it had not happened (which was a hundred thousand to one) that the ship floated from the place where she first struck and was driven so near to the shore that I had time to get all these things out of her.

> What would have been my case if I had been forced to have lived in the condition in which I at first came on shore, without necessaries of life, or necessaries to supply and procure them?

Bereft of company, he is consoled by the "necessaries" of life—his things.

Completely removed from marketplace logic, Crusoe appreciates his things for their use value alone. Every object in his little compound takes on a heightened significance: "I found the carpenter's chest, which was indeed a very useful prize to me, and much more valuable than a ship-lading of gold would have been at that time." And use value is not just applied to tools. Crusoe also finds ink, pen, and paper on the ship, "of less value, but not at all less useful to me." Usefulness, it seems, even on a desert island, includes things that aid Crusoe in living a contemplative life. The pen and ink become a means to reflection. He immediately begins to make lists and to keep a journal. Completely isolated, removed from civilization, Crusoe remains in history. No noble savage is he, for he has things, and therefore the need to keep accounts, to write, and to mark his existence.

I read Defoe's novel for the first time at twenty-five, the year my mother died. I had moved far away from my parents to live with S. while he went to graduate school. He was busy and I felt friendless, abandoned to my grief. My world had shrunk to the size of our apartment, and to the few things I had rescued from my past. Now there was no going back. Feeling shipwrecked, I could not condescend to Crusoe nor mock his fearful relationship to the "other." All my domestic attempts felt akin to his solitary re-creation of home and habits on his Island of Despair. Strange how fragile it feels to "play house" once you can no longer go home.

As a child I had loved playing house, especially in wild spaces. I remember in particular a low gnarled tree whose branches curved over to form a little room complete with convenient bark-lined seats. I would fill little interiors such as this with cozy, domestic rituals. I would pretend I was alone, cut off from the world, but underneath my made-up scenarios I always knew I was safe, and that the comforts of my parents' house could be accessed at any moment (though often I packed a first-aid kit, just in case). No matter how remote I imagined my circumstance —how little my house, how big the woods—I would replicate order and ritual, for what is wildness without a witness? I understood completely why Crusoe, despite his solitude and the intense heat of the island, could not bring himself to go naked. Rebellious acts are for stuffy rooms, not wilderness outposts.

The risk: I learned that older boys attuned to social power could destroy the magic of even my most fortified structures with only a passing laugh. Perhaps this is why I found Crusoe's panic at the legendary footprint, while charmingly comic, understandable. In an economy of one, value is not visible, locked as it is in a single imagination, which has, without sanction or public notice, transformed an unassuming hovel into an entire world. And yet the "owner" of what looks to be an unenviable fort, having all his or her existence bound up there, cannot fathom the possibility that others may not covet it. Crusoe's love for his things filled him with the terror of losing them. Proof positive for Plato: loving things not only distracts us from the Beautiful and the Good, it turns us into potential victims and fills us with fear of our would-be friends.

We should get over it. If, that is, we hope to unlock the mysteries of love and reach the Beautiful and the Good. This must be done carefully, by slow, steep, hierarchical steps. Or so Socrates tells us, having gained this mystical knowledge from the priestess Diotima.

If we rise above our love for beautiful things, we shall free ourselves from death and decay, from beauty's transience and our acquisitive nature. We shall fear no footprint. But in order to reach this state of tranquility, we must work our way up to the beauty that is "unmixed, not adulterated with human flesh and colors and much other mortal rubbish." A beauty without sensuality, which can only be perceived with the mind. A beauty, therefore, that cannot exist in the "things we live among." Or can it?

Is this a pure idealism? A doctrine meant to teach disdain for and fear of the material world? What André-Jean Festugière would call a "pessimist gnosis"? Or are "mortal rubbish" and "human flesh" important components of this philosophical quest?

According to Socrates, it is through our love for *real things* that we first are able to glimpse the ideal. In this *The Symposium* differs from the culture of Christian asceticism: the material world is not evil. Rather, it *participates* in the Beautiful. It is as if there is a zone of rarefied air—Beauty itself—that objects pass through, and while bathed in its eternal particles, they give us a glimpse of Beauty itself. If we do not fall in love with the world, we shall never know the ideal that infuses it. An optimist gnosis?

Not quite . . .

For this rarefied air works its magic differently on different matter. Over flesh and bone it seems to hover only briefly. On art and in Nature it lingers much longer, sometimes for many millennia. Despite these illusions we must never forget that Beauty does not emanate from the material world. It is not immanent.

She who understands this will climb to the top rung of Diotima's ladder, and then kick it out from under her. She will no longer be subject to the mineral fact. She will "touch reality," not its pale semblance. And it will be granted to her "to be the friend of God, and immortal if any man ever is." A direct wormhole to the divine. No rituals, trinkets, or icons, just a straight mental shot right to the source.

THE REALITY IS MORE EXCELLENT THAN THE REPORT

Sleepy Hollow Cemetery, Concord, Massachusetts: after hiking a small hill I come upon a humble marker, no more than a foot or so high, which simply reads "HENRY." It is bedecked with the stones, acorns, feathers, and pinecones. Delightful. A little further on I find a different sort of marker. A large and powerful wave of rough-hewn granite juts from the earth, looking as though shaped by no hand other than that of Nature herself. The verdigris plaque embedded in the rock reads:

RALPH WALDO EMERSON
BORN IN BOSTON MAY 25 1803
DIED IN CONCORD APRIL 27 1882

THE PASSIVE MASTER LENT HIS HAND
TO THE VAST SOUL THAT OER HIM PLANNED

A "vast soul" indeed. A soul embodied in granite, from a man who wrote, "It is a long way from granite to the oyster; farther yet to Plato and the preaching of the immortality of the soul. Yet all must come, as surely as the first atom has two sides."

In the hands of this "passive master," Nature is no pale semblance, nor is it something against which "The power of the mind . . . Is not enough." Rather, "world is mind precipitated." Mind and thing are in constant colloquy: "the volatile essence [of the world] is forever escaping again into the state of free thought. Hence the virtue and pungency of the influence on the mind of natural objects." No ideas but in things. Yes. But take it further: ideas escape things, as electrons the atom. The world is a quivering intelligence that we "penetrate bodily . . . we dip our hands in this painted element; our eyes are bathed in these lights and forms."

Then why, in the midst of this somatic immersion, is "Nature . . . still elsewhere," and why does the poet feel distanced from his object? Is philosophy to blame? Or the condition of being numerous? There is a deep solitude in Emerson's immersion: "We come to our own, and make friends with matter, which the ambitious chatter of the schools would persuade us to despise."

Perhaps, from an evolutionary perspective, our philosophy's anxious positing of eternals arises not from a wish to still the dizzying pace of one meager life, but from a longing to witness the slow changes Nature authors. Natural objects seem indifferent to us, and we envy their "cool, disengaged air." By despising the material life we mimic this indifference, and say to Nature, in effect, *we do not need you to be happy.*

We fear Nature's "friction"—the impulse it includes in all things that excites the energies and keeps the world moving. In our vain attempts to remove it, to stop things, to see and preserve them, we wall them up, we order them: "This palace of brick and stone, these servants, this kitchen, these stables, horses and equipage, this bank-stock and file of mortgages; trade to all the world . . . all for a little conversation, high, clear, and spiritual!" Is this conversation our philosophy? And is philosophy, therefore, a child of the city? Perhaps. And yet, as Emerson tells us, cities are no more removed from Nature than we are removed from our primal instincts: "If we had eyes to see it, a bit of stone from the city wall would certify us of the necessity that man must exist, as readily as the city."

The same living signature that draws the eyes of Oppen's city dwellers to the surrounding bricks is embedded in Emerson's granite avatar, his "bit of stone." Though for this citizen of Sleepy Hollow Cemetery, Nature—the mineral fact—is neither melancholic nor alienating. It is a place where "wisdom is infused into every form" and "Beauty breaks in everywhere."

Mr. Tulliver, the ruined mill-owner of George Eliot's *The Mill on the Floss,* has fallen into a state of delirium, verging on comatose. He does not recognize his own son. At one point he briefly emerges from his stupor and becomes clear and alert. The cause: the sound of his desk, a cherished heirloom. His son and brother-in-law are rifling through it looking for a promissory note. The sound of an object has succeeded where the voices of his loved ones failed. Eliot explains: "All long-known objects, even a mere window-fastening or a particular door-latch, have sounds which are a sort of recognized voice to us—a voice that will thrill and awaken, when it has been used to touch deep-lying fibres." Mr. Tulliver, who has lived in the same house since boyhood, feels oriented by the sound of his things. They extend and guard his selfhood.

Roland Barthes understands this. In his essay "Listening" he links our ability to hear to our "spatio-temporal situation." We hear around corners and through walls. "Alert" listening takes place when we attempt to decipher unfamiliar sounds. It is a primal animal act that arouses our "deep-lying fibres." It is connected to fear and love.

Unless technology intervenes (the telephone, for example), sound and space are intimately connected. Whether we live in a single-family home or in an apartment surrounded by tenants, we make an aural map of the customary sounds. Barthes again: "Domestic space . . . is a space of familiar, *recognized* noises whose ensemble forms a kind of household symphony." Barthes's symphony rewrites Oppen's lines to read "There are things / We live among and to *hear* them / Is to know we are safe." Unfamiliar sounds alert us to the possibility of danger, of something amiss in our environment. The sound of footsteps under a window where no one should be walking, the sudden creaking in a basement, someone rifling through a private desk, our eyes may close in sleep, but our ears stay open to protect us.

A first night's sleep in a new place is often a white night of sonic mapping. There is no way to distinguish easily an innocuous from a dangerous noise. Every sound must be physically investigated, its origin determined and settled. But what if you find yourself in a stranger's home, where such "investigations" would be suspect?

Such is the dilemma I find myself in, age eighteen, on the first night of my second au pair post. The family I have come to work for (mother, two boys) lives in a small apartment on the eighth floor of a high rise. My tiny room is dominated by a double bed. The headboard is flush against a floor-to-ceiling sliding glass door that opens onto a concrete balcony too slim to actually stand on. Before I retire for the night, my French woman shows me how to lower the heavy horizontal blind down over the glass. Turning the wand, I lock the segmented slats of the snaky blind into place, obliterating the lights from the apartment-complex parking lot. The room is in total darkness.

A storm comes up. The wind, whipping through the air, jangles the formidable blind. I am awakened by the noise and then, for what seems like hours, I lie petrified in the darkness, certain that someone, or *something*, is tapping against the blind, demanding entry. I turn my vigil into a Poe story. Finally, courage mustered, I wake my employer. New to my situation, I am unaware that she is a troubled sleeper who, once awakened, will stay up until morning. She is stiff with rage. She finds the illogic of my fear intolerable. How stupid must I be to think that a prowler would scale a high rise to rattle some blinds?

Gripped as I was by the strangeness of my surroundings, in an apartment with people I have only just met, reason took no part in my fear. The strange inexplicable sounds created a strange world, a world in which building heights were irrelevant, and evil forces, unleashed by the disruption of my ability to read the sounds, lurked in the perfectly innocuous materials of a small post-war apartment.

Technology can introduce foreign sounds into our "spatio-temporal situation." Near the end of *The Magic Mountain,* Thomas Mann illustrates how uncanny imported sound can be. He draws a subtle line from meditating on a miraculous technological object to contemplating the mysteries of the mind.

From the section called "Fullness of Harmony": A new amusement appears in the common room of the sanatorium. Mann, attuned to the power of a good build up, writes two generous paragraphs before revealing the nature of the object: "since we ourselves are much taken by that mysterious object's secret charms. . . ." It is a gramophone. But not just *any* gramophone, no "wretched crank-box . . . the sort of thing you might have found . . . set up on a tavern counter to fill unsophisticated ears with nasal braying." It is, rather, the "newest model," electric, and in a sleek black box with a "gracefully beveled lid." All of the residents are enchanted. Hans Castorp, however, falls farther than even enchantment into the deepest love. He develops a strange empathy with the device. Worried the other patients will abuse it, he proclaims himself its sole operator, eventually pocketing the key to the gramophone's cabinet and store of records, so that anyone who desires to listen must appeal to him. The others, more interested in the music than the device that produces it, accept this arrangement.

For several nights Hans Castorp stays up late listening to records in the common room. While sleeping he dreams of "his magic box." In his dream he sees the "turntable whirling around its spindle, so fast it became invisible, inaudible, not simply rotating wildly in place, but moving in a strange lateral undulation so that the arm beneath which it turned began to oscillate supplely, as if it were breathing ..." The miraculous object is possessed of a lifelike aura; it is a phantom, a "truncated coffin" that plays "ghostly" music: "The vibrations produced amazing effects near their source, but like all ghostly things, quickly languished with distance, grew feeble, their powers merely illusory." The recorded singers, as though haunting the room, can be heard but not seen. Their bodies, far from the sanatorium, "resided in America, in Milan, in Vienna . . ."

The gramophone's power to conjure voices transforms Hans Castorp. Listening to the room fill with sound, he imagines himself as a Pan-like figure, with legs of a goat and pipes of reed. Then the gramophone unlocks the very mysteries of life. It brings him into a mystical convergence with Schubert's "Der Lindenbaum," behind the forbidden love of which he senses the world of death. To express the significance of this song, Mann includes his definition of a successful work of art:

> an object created by the human spirit and intellect, which means a significant object, is 'significant' in that it points beyond itself, is an expression and exponent of a more universal spirit and intellect, of a whole world of feelings and ideas that have found a more or less perfect image of themselves in that object . . .

Where does Mann's story go, following his meditation on the miraculous gramophone? To the unconscious, to the "dark, vast regions of the human soul." The method of travel? Hypnosis, telepathy, séances. But no matter how esoteric things become, they always lead back to the material world, for "any man who recognizes an organic symptom of illness to be the product of forbidden emotions that assume hysterical form in conscious psychic life also recognizes the creative power of the psyche in the material world."

A new patient from Denmark, a plain flaxen-haired girl, is discovered to be a telepath. One of the research doctors begins to use her in his occult experiments with states of consciousness. A select group of long-term sanatorium residents join in these secret séances. Like Hans Castorp with the gramophone, a few become obsessed. Soon it is discovered that music aids the telepath, and the gramophone is brought into the laboratory. Even after his precious machine is requisitioned, Hans Castorp resists these activities. He feels superior to them. Then one night, pressed by the other participants, who have excitedly told him that they have succeeded in conjuring the dead, Hans Castorp gives in.

What follows are "the strangest hours" in the young hero's life. After an agonizing and drawn-out séance, aided by the disembodied music of the gramophone, the spirit of Hans Castorp's recently deceased cousin, Joachim Ziemssen, appears. Appalled at his role in conjuring the apparition and horrified by what he sees, Hans whispers "forgive me" to the sad wraith of his emaciated cousin, and, as the gramophone needle on the record "scratche[s] idly in the silence," he turns on the lights and exits the room.

Maman has had a fall. She is in her late seventies and lives alone in her apartment in Paris. Over two hours she crawls along the floor to reach the phone. Rescued by neighbors, she is taken to the hospital. She will not return home. A cancer is discovered, and then, after an operation, the body of Françoise de Beauvoir slowly decays away from life. Her final weeks are chronicled in open-eyed and sober detail by her daughter Simone in the memoir *A Very Easy Death*.

After *Maman* dies, Simone and her sister Poupette must clear out her hospital room: "As we looked at her straw bag, filled with balls of wool and an unfinished piece of knitting, and at her blotting-pad, her scissors, her thimble, emotion rose up and drowned us." Confronting a piece of black ribbon, Poupette begins to cry: "It's so stupid and I'm not at all a worshipper of things, but I just can't throw this ribbon away."

De Beauvoir comments on this scene with a statement

that reflects her Proustian inheritance: "Everyone knows the power of things: life is solidified in them, more immediately present than in any one of its instants." Though I feel great sympathy with this statement, I still question it. Does "everyone" really know this? Or is the death of someone close to you necessary to "solidify" illusive life into otherwise common, everyday things? Things whose owner has died, things that, de Beauvoir admits, are "waiting to turn into rubbish or to find another identity"?

Two in particular solidified my mother's life for me: a rectangular tortoise-shell magnifying glass with a broken handle, and a grayish-white hair brush with alternating rows of black and white bristles, many bent; two odd objects, both of which she should have replaced. Why these two out of all of the things that belonged to her? A mystery. Some of her things embarrassed me, baffled as I was by her enthusiasm for them (corn-husk dollies). Others, though I knew they were *hers,* managed to return to a state of generic anonymity after she was gone. Most of her clothes fell into this category. But the brush and the magnifying glass destroyed me. I did not question their power. I took them home with me and stored them in busily trafficked nooks.

The brush went in a drawer with my own brushes and cosmetics. Every day when I did my make-up, the sight of it surprised me, as if I wasn't sure how it got there. It gave me a feeling of nervous transgression, like I had felt as a girl when I looked through my mother's toiletries. It wasn't forbidden but for some reason felt so: as if I feared I might find some secret that would work to deflate her awesome power. The difference was that the nervous feeling now arose from a crushing sense of guilt. The brush said: she is dead. A fact I kept trying to deny.

I stored the magnifying glass in the top drawer of my Lady's Desk. It wasn't always immediately visible until I rifled about. It reminded me of my childhood fascination with the "tools" connected to my mother's intellect: glasses, a paper cutter, a box of tissue (for hygiene, not crying), and this glass, which she used to look up words in Webster's New International.

Twenty years later these objects no longer hold the same pathos as they did right after she died. I no longer tear up at their touch. Yet they have never become mine. Next to the myriad "rubbish" in which my own life has solidified, they still bespeak another's.

THING MEMORY

In the overture to *The Search for Lost Time*, Proust describes the first of the narrator's several experiences of *mémoire involontaire*. The oft-quoted scene: after taking a spoonful of tea mixed with the crumbs of a *petite madeleine*:

> No sooner had the warm liquid mixed with the crumbs touched my palate than a shudder ran through me . . . An exquisite pleasure had invaded my senses . . . And at once the vicissitudes of life had become indifferent to me, its disasters innocuous, its brevity illusory . . . I had ceased now to feel mediocre, contingent, mortal.

The sensation is so powerful it physically transforms the narrator and dissolves the limits of materiality: time and decay, contingency and mortality are no more. By making his gateway the *senses*—provoked by a material thing —Proust distinguishes his route to transcendence from

Plato's. Here dialectical reason will not help you. The sensual route, more akin to grace, cannot be controlled or reproduced, not even through mental discipline. It is involuntary. Over and over again the narrator dips the *petite madeleine* into the tea and tastes the warm liquid, but each subsequent attempt only works to diminish the portal opened by the initial dip.

The *petite madeleine* does not house the narrator's short-lived feeling. It is only the catalyst for a sensation. The sensation unlocks a moment from the past, which, *in the past*, had no particular significance. Yet in memory this same moment becomes the key to a cascade of detailed memories of a place long forgotten: Combray. Proust shows us how seemingly banal experiences have the ability to pocket a folded quantum of "timeless essence" into our unconscious. This essence may be activated by a chance interaction with an object at an unknown point in the future, or it may lie dormant our entire lives.

The things Proust privileges as triggers are often banal, daily things (a public restroom, a napkin, a paving stone), things one might encounter hundreds of times without experiencing *mémoire involontaire*. Thus the object world's power to release the human mind from its temporal and material prison is not just a matter of replication. It is a complex orchestration involving a highly specific and unreproducible interaction between human bodies and material things.

In Proust, things need not be specific to you (a toy from childhood) or precious (an heirloom) to provoke *mémoire involontaire.* Mass production does not impoverish them. The sensual experience they provoke floats free of them, settling at will on the changing object world. And thus, as long as there are analogs that can provoke the old sensations, our access to transcendence is not threatened by the decay or destruction of our material past:

> But when from a long-distant past nothing subsists, after the people are dead, after the things are broken and scattered, taste and smell alone, more fragile but more enduring, more unsubstantial, more persistent, more faithful, remain poised a long time, like souls, remembering, waiting, hoping, amid the ruins of all the rest; and bear unflinchingly, in the tiny and almost impalpable drop of their essence, the vast structure of recollection.

Taste and smell are privileged over sight, touch, and sound. They have the same ability to conjure the dead as Hans Castorp's gramophone.

By taking the ability to conjure memory out of our hands, Proust provides an explanation for why our attempts to recapture it by returning to a childhood home or neighborhood, or by cooking some maternal dish, often feel futile and empty, more estranging than revelatory. We return to places and things looking for our past, but it is not there. And when this happens we call ourselves unfeeling, or worry that we have lost the essence of ourselves to the crass concerns of adulthood. But we need not fear. Our past is in us, locked away, waiting to be released by some seemingly innocuous material thing, a trigger of a sensual experience that will make us "shudder."

*

Providence, Rhode Island: S. and I have rented an apartment on the second floor of a house. The house is old, and the stairwell, stained a deep walnut, turns around a large newel. Summer heat releases the wood's humidity, and the sticky treads cling to their dust. One morning I open the door and walk down these stairs to get the mail. I crouch to gather the limp envelopes from the floor and I am there: in the two-hundred-year-old French farmhouse where I spent four of the most miserable months of my young life. It is my first au pair job. I work for a dismal young couple with two toddlers. The *friteuse,* the yelling, the jarred béarnaise, the shelf of *Harlequin* romances, the ram's charge, the drowned kittens, the feral children, all materialize in the smell of the wood. It is an old, dark smell. European.

Unlike Combray for Proust's narrator, this exceptional episode was not trapped in my distant past. It had been only eight years ago. I could remember what happened, but not what it felt like. The *mémoire involontaire* collapsed time, dissolving the dispassion of my memory's narrative. It was not a set of details but a shudder. I was *in* that farmhouse, outside of identity, outside of English, alone, and wondering why I couldn't go home. This transport did not free me from feeling "mediocre, contingent, mortal," but rather made me feel these things all the more. For a moment, I was sealed in a melancholy wave. But then I thought: I'm not there, I'm here, in Providence, in a life of my choosing, mistress of my own set of circumstances. In the wash of my relief, the thin film of sensual memory was no longer a threat; rather, I saw how it could add a patina of charm to my erstwhile experience. I could have that time back, without being trapped in the negative circumstance. This is *mémoire involontaire*'s gift—as well as poetry's.

Proust shows us how the sensations of taste and smell can unlock a vivid memory, but what about sight? Does the visual store? Or is it a sense that functions only in the present tense, and abstractly, apart from the sensuousness of things?

We can see pictures in the mind in dreams, or when we call up a memory, but are these visions of our "mind's eye" accurate records of experience, or are they something else altogether? Childhood homes, revisited in thought a thousand times, often turn out to be smaller and dingier than we remember. Our visual record of them ill matches their material fact. The sight archive, like the dream work, is warped by psychological rearrangement. It turns our memories into abstract symbols, not accurate records of actual space.

As my older body moves through the locales my younger body negotiated, frame by frame the images in my mind are replaced by the real-time experience of seeing in the here and now. The street I grew up on is relatively unchanged, but on return visits it never *looks* right. The slope of the hill is less steep, the length and width considerably off. Yet the eucalyptus and pepper trees smell perfect, completely undistorted by time. Is this because I cannot reproduce these smells through mental exercise as I can the visual field?

Film images are not affected by memory's distorted visual archive. Movies can be remembered accurately. Perhaps this is because film offers us a visual experience unlike any other: isolated, simplified, aesthetic. It activates only two senses: sight and hearing. No matter how ambulatory the camera, the film is flat and excludes the body, which sits passively, locked in a chair. Film makes love to the eye by relieving it of its duty to negotiate space so it can accurately record what it sees, at last.

SADDLE

After my stepfather—the last of my parents—dies, my older brother and I must clean out our childhood home. We have a deadline: two weeks. I must return to graduate school in the East, he to work. An added pressure comes from our stepsiblings, who want to sell the house as quickly as possible. The circumstance makes me feel a bit like Crusoe, trying to rescue as many "necessaries" from the ship as I can before it sinks.

In the front closet, which runs between my old bedroom and my mother's office, I find it. My saddle. It is an English saddle, a Stübben, resting over the back of my mother's sewing-machine case. I have not used it on a regular basis since I was fourteen years old, when I quit riding and showing "for good." But what am I saying? Commitment in my family was such that there were no casual hobbies. Quitting "for good" was okay when it came to relationships with people, not interests. Interests were innate definers of personality. To lay aside a toy, a book, a desire, to "lose interest" showed a fundamental weakness of character. In defiance I became quite the dilettante. I was a pianist, a guitarist, a painter, a producer of grand opera, and so on.

But riding was different. Before I became interested in boys, it was my true passion. I recycled millions of tin cans and delivered hundreds of newspapers to indulge it. Every weekend my mom would drive me to the stable— some forty minutes away. My saddle would straddle a towel draped on the back seat of "Lolly," our Volkswagen camper van. Once placed on whichever horse I was currently riding—*Stilts*, *Top Notch*, *Peepers*—it transformed me into a wholly different creature. Girls and women tend not to have places that are theirs to "sit." They perch here and there, on the edges, accommodating. This was my seat, formed to my young body, perfect for me. No one else had access to it. In my saddle I was tall, neat, dignified. Slouch dissolved, posture impeccable.

When we packed up to leave the stable my saddle would be encrusted with horse sweat. Once home I would wash it with sudsy saddle soap, then oil it with linseed oil. The smells brought me back to the stable, and to the deep animal freedom of the horses that helped me go fast, fast enough so that my body could follow the pulse of my spirit.

Now in a new phase of life, what am I to do with this magical portal masquerading as layered scallops of soft brown leather? Convinced that my interest in riding and horses is innate, and therefore bound to return, I send the saddle home. When I go abroad I put it in storage. When I return stateside I take it out of storage. When I buy a house in Maine I sit it on the back of the balustrade that runs around the stairwell on the upstairs landing. By this point the saddle's leather is dusty and dry. Cobwebs creep over its folds. No one has sat in it for years. My saddle surprises me anew each time I climb the stairs to the half-floor, usually when giving a house tour to a friend, who inevitably asks about the saddle. The saddle seems to require a story, a story I have lost all interest in telling. "Oh, that's *my* saddle," I say—as though they would have thought it belonged to S.—and then I move on to the next room.

Thirty years after "dismounting" for good, eight years after moving to Maine, S. and I are sorting through old things, trying to bring order to the layers of objects we have collected, inherited, found. My saddle sits quietly by. Its weathered leather, strong "irons," straight straps, and suede knee pads betray the increasingly rare quality of a well-crafted thing, a thing that cannot be thrown away, no matter how old and worn, without disrespecting the hidden history of the human hands that made it. Old wooden tools carry the same *gravitas*. But is not disuse a similar offense?

I finally decide: I will give my saddle to the ailing stable down the street. "Perhaps they can get some use out of it." A few days later, alone in the house, I pick up the saddle and tuck my right arm under it. Halfway to the car the feel of the saddle straddling my arm unlocks a wave of sadness. All that has been abandoned "for good"—my beloved horses, my equestrian hopes, my commitment—returns. As I set the saddle awkwardly on its side in the trunk of the car, the betrayed life looks back.

Looking at objects from a partitioned distance can be oddly frustrating. Or so it has been my experience in decorative-arts museums, where one is asked to walk "in front of" rooms you cannot enter, and look from a distance at empty beds, desks, tea and coffee services, duck presses (?), etc. that you cannot sleep on, write at, drink from, or . . . (I assume) press a duck in. There is something tawdry and sad about the whole affair, gazing at threadbare silk upholstery and dusty tapestry from past royalty while trying to conjure splendor, looking at silverware through glass without knowing the weight of it in the hand, the feel of it on the tongue.

Painting and sculpture are made to be self-contained, but practical things, even if beautifully designed, need a context. And to really make sense they need the people who valued and used them. Without their owners such things take on a pathos; they turn from coveted and comforting objects to mere curiosities, examples of past fashions that we, bloated with contemporary hubris, feel proud to have left behind: "How could anyone have slept in such a ridiculous bed!" "Isn't this silverware garish," and so on.

One of the saddest Thing Museums of all is the fingerprint-stained glass display case next to the cash register of most thrift stores. Underneath the case's protection lie mid-priced jewelry and odd trinkets of the recent past, usually arranged by color and type: clip-on earrings with chipped gold and blue paint, bent baby spoons, broken lockets, faux-pearl necklaces missing pearls. Unlike the generically uniformed museum guards in national decorative-arts museums, the workers in thrift shops are typically of a piece with their wares—an aged member of the blue-rinse set impeccably dressed and coiffed in yesterday's latest; or perhaps a youthful re-interpreter of the same look, whose pale skin and dyed black hair provocatively contrast with musty taffeta and bright lipstick.

Watched over by these self-appointed mannequins of the forgotten world, you look for treasures. You try to attach a wayward and fickle sense of value to the objects lying passively in the display case. But, like a poem out of context, they cause intense value anxiety. Are they junk?

Treasures? Well or poorly made? How do you know? That they are locked in a case *should*, it seems, count for something. You are brought back to basics—materials, craftsmanship, form, and the whims of imagination. Inevitably, your admiration for the fact that such seemingly valueless things have survived is mixed with sad thoughts of their erstwhile owners. In what forgotten plot of land do they lie? Before that fact these abandoned things are mute. They will not give up their stories.

A dear friend is diagnosed with a rare cancer. A few months later, before I have even processed the news, she is dead. She is twenty-eight. I ask her widower, also a friend, for a memento or two. I have photographs, but I want something more, something in three dimensions that I can hold in my hand. She was a writer and I'm thinking of writerly things, a notebook, a pen, or perhaps a favorite volume of poems with her name on the flyleaf and her quizzical notes in the margins. A short while later a small package arrives in the mail. In it I find the following: one half-used bottle of Cutex Perfect Color for Nails in "wicked white frost"; one reddish plastic decorative hair comb; one large safety pin; one plastic tortoiseshell-colored purse mirror, rectangular, with the mirror scratched and the tain damaged; one necklace, a pendant on a chain with red and blue rhinestones in a star/flower pattern; one silver ring with a greenish stone; one trinket ring, probably from one of those dispensers that have "prizes" in plastic eggs located at the checkout of many diners; one foil section from a package of Sine-Aid with one pill missing; one rolodex card reading "Juno 281-7966." And that is it.

Though at first I am baffled by this gathering of odd and apparently worthless things, I gradually began to understand the profundity of the widower's gesture, to see what he could see from across the gender divide: that my friendship with his wife, though ostensibly a literary one, was actually built—as all great female friendships are —on an uncritical acceptance, even admiration, of the other's way of inhabiting her gender. These "leftovers" of a lovely and strong adult woman were nothing more than the trinkets of a girl on the brink of puberty, that time when the things that bespeak femininity become the coveted objects of fantasy. Each broken and tarnished piece looked weary from the crushing weight of desire that had doubtless been heaped upon its fragile construction.

What will be the appropriate home for my newly acquired treasures? A little padded box. This one, covered in black satin printed with little white stars, came long ago from an enchanting gift shop called The Paper Moon. The lid is decorated with a felt cutout of a friendly half-moon and a star. I wore a silver ring with the same motif all through junior high—my "moons and stars" period. The box ties shut with a white ribbon, which has become quite grungy over the years. Into its cushioned confines go my girlfriend's things, a soft home for the young hopes of a woman denied the time to fulfill them.

1982. On my way to spend a year as an au pair in France. I begin with a few "literary" weeks in England. Before setting off on my own to Bath (Austen) and Dorset (Hardy), I spend a couple of days with family friends in the London suburb of Harrow. A kind middle-class family of four. The father is an historian who, having discovered my bent for old things, invites me to accompany him to the weekly Harrow Market in search of treasures.

The July day is bright, but not so hot as to spoil the mood. My literary imagination is much activated by wandering through the booths, my eyes moving from baffling curios to well-crafted household objects that, each in its own way, conjure up some romanticized vision of well-ordered interiors and the quotidian pleasures of the industrious domestic routines of the past. The smells of linseed oil and saddle soap permeate the air. My host, a dedicated collector (his household décor owes much to the beautiful but practical things of the previous century—no chintz or frills), heads purposefully off, allowing me to drift at my own pace. Though I desire much, I am limited by my pocketbook, as well as by the fact that I am a traveler and cannot acquire more than I can carry. My two bags, one small and one large, are already rather stuffed, packed as they are for a full year of life.

I then see, flowing softly in the breeze, several full-length garments hanging in haphazard fashion on a wire cord above cracked and painful-looking boots, the dimensions of which make me wonder if the past hundred years have seen an inexplicably speedy evolution in the typical size of the female foot. Approaching the booth, my desire lights on an antique nightgown. It is thick white cotton muslin trimmed with an inch of soft thick lace (almost like kitchen string) edging the square-cut collar and cuffs. Shopping for antiques with an historian and collector presents a rare opportunity for "authentication," and so, before parting with my pounds, which I hardly know the value of, I head off to find my host.

He is quickly recovered and proclaims the purchase sound on two important grounds: charm and imaginative fancy. And it was fairly priced.

That evening, after a nice warm bath, I put on my new old nightgown and, with a cup of tea beside me, climb up into the high squeaky brass bed in the cozy guest room. The mood is incomparable. I open my journal and ready my pen to exact a perfect *old manuscript* hand, when a soft rap comes at the door. Somehow I know that the intrusion, though irregular, will not spoil the scenario: the aura of the objects involved is too strong, and the mood's centerpiece, the antique nightgown, is too powerful a conjurer to quiver at what is certain to be a negligible interruption.

"Yes," I say, attempting to approximate the obliging voice of an appreciative guest.

Very slowly the door opens, and from the dark hallway the ambient light of a kerosene lamp enters the room, carried by my host whose face, framed by his reddish beard, looks pleased and somewhat childlike, as if he is participating in a truly satisfying game of pretend. "I thought this just might suit your attire," he says. Placing the lamp on the bedside table, he quietly backs out of the room.

CLOTHES

A friend, in a mostly positive email response to my memoir *The Middle Room,* adds: "maybe I now know more than I need about people's clothes . . ." I laugh when reading this. Yes, perhaps such "trivial" details need not be included in the story of one's artistic development.

There is a legendary story about my grandmother, Frances Moxley, who died before I was born. Near the end of her life, confined to bed, this elegant woman who had always struggled to "keep her figure" was thin and frail, dying of stomach cancer. Her daughter-in-law, my mother Jo, was her final caretaker.

Frances, knowing she does not have long to live, asks Jo a favor. "Will you go into my closet, take out each of my fine dresses, and bring them over by the bedside where I can see them?"

What for? My mother wonders.

To bid each one farewell. Piece by piece my grandmother says goodbye to her wardrobe.

My mother told me this story repeatedly, always in a tone of delighted superiority, as if pleased to have her prejudices against Frances confirmed by the gift of this ridiculous, parting gesture. "She was dying and she thought about her clothes!" my mother would exclaim.

When our bodies are failing, is it necessary that we despise them, scorning former adornments and physical pleasures? When my own mother was dying I remember her picking up a cat and burying her nose in the soft pelt. "I love the smell of a cat's fur," she said, a simple pleasure into which all of life's sensuous joys seemed at that moment to concentrate.

*

At no time is the personal, intimate nature of clothes felt more strongly than when borrowing or lending them. Every teenage girl who wraps herself in the leather jacket of her beau knows this. The item of borrowed clothing carries the smell of its owner, its ill-fit gives you a curious awareness of your body, like being in someone else's skin. Lending a signature item out of love is of course different from lending a generic item out of need.

A glamorous woman poet, known for her theatrical

style, comes to give a reading at my university. Her luggage is lost. Clearly upset, she laughs it off in order to set her hosts at ease. May I borrow a toothbrush, something to sleep in, and some clean underwear? Underwear? Really? I do not question it. Luckily, the intimacy of the item gets lost in the loan. This is a practical request, not a personal one. Any connection between the underwear and my identity must be downplayed. By rights I shouldn't *loan* my panties, but rather an extra pair that don't yet belong to anyone. But while I keep extra toothbrushes on hand, I do not have a closet filled with unused "emergency" panties. I pick a scarcely worn, fairly new pair that I don't have any particular fondness for. I find the thought of someone out there, a fellow poet, wearing my panties a bit embarrassing. Though she agrees to return the pair by mail, some loans, though neither party speaks of it, are tacitly understood to be gifts.

NECCHI WEEP

Standard-sized shower curtains do not fit the odd-sized shower stall in our bathroom. They must be cut down and hemmed. I buy a yellow fabric one, which is pricey, no doubt because it is part of the "Hotel Collection." As I gravitate toward it, I wonder if the old-fashioned positive connotations of home are no longer marketable in "commodity hell" (as S. calls the Mall). Once "home cooking" was a restaurant's boldest claim. Now restaurant-style cooking done in "professional" kitchens is the *ne plus ultra* of the home cook ... or should I say "chef"? Hotels used to brag that they could make you feel at home. Now we drape our homey beds in linens extolled as "hotel quality." Has capitalism managed to make the idea of home shabby? Turned "homemade" into an embarrassment? Robbing us of our self-reliance and ingenuity? Our ability to economize by doing it ourselves? Or is this phenomenon merely a reflection of a cultural change? When everyone has to work nobody is left to tend the homestead. "Home" becomes just a place you visit briefly in the evenings . . . like a hotel. It should be clean and anonymous, and have a generic bed fitted with fine-quality linen that you can leave without regret.

I associate homemade things with childhood. My mother made almost all of my clothes. A-line dresses and jumpers, a Christmas dress of wine-colored velvet with white lace sleeves. I remember the excitement of sitting next to her at the big communal table at the back of the fabric store leafing through pattern books. They were my first fashion magazines, filled with beautiful models and dream clothing. But none of it had to be bought, it could all be *made*, and to fit. My favorite was a jumper she made me of cream corduroy with a repeated pattern of Siamese cats. I wore it over a chocolate turtleneck to dramatic effect. My mother even made my bathing suits. As I grew I had several generations of a bright-red two-piece she thought "absolutely adorable." The top had a white plastic ring in the middle. When I started show jumping, shocked at the cost of riding clothes, she tackled the challenge of making my kit: the result, an elegant hunter-green jacket with three gold buttons, worn over sleek white stretchy breeches.

My mother taught me the basics of hand sewing, and when I was old enough, initiated me into the ease and pleasure of sewing on her machine. She was very proud of it. It was Italian, a Necchi. She taught me how to thread the machine before sewing, to guide the thread through the baroque mechanical maze from spindle to needle: around this knob, through that metal bracket, between these two slits, behind this clip, and finally through the eye of the needle itself. She also taught me how to load a bobbin, and how to make the magical turns that dip the needle down below to retrieve the thread from its brother bobbin. Empty bobbins could be rethreaded on the far-right side of the Necchi. After switching to "bobbin mode" and guiding the thread through another complex path, this time from spindle to bobbin, you could fill the small metal spool with the color of your choice in seconds.

My mother didn't sew much after I hit puberty. I could do my own sewing by this time anyway, and many were the wide-legged pants I "pegged" in service to my manias for retro-inspired looks. But I did not have the patience to be an ambitious seamstress, and my mother's prized sewing machine was often silent during these years. Once I left home, it never occurred to me to buy my own. I eschewed complex sewing projects and hemmed my pants by hand. It was as if her Necchi was the only machine there ever was or would be. A reliable, irreplaceable object, which did, when my mother died, become mine.

When I inherited the Necchi, it had lain so long without use that it needed a tune-up. I took it to Mr. Spirito, an old Italian man with a small shop in Federal Hill, the Italian neighborhood of Providence. Mr. Spirito confirmed my sense of its greatness, saying, "Necchi's are the best-made sewing machines in the world." He returned my mother's to me in fine working order. That was almost twenty years ago.

*

The shower curtain is yellow. The bobbin is threaded with red. I prepare to spool over it with a cotton thread the color of egg yolks whisked with sugar. S. is washing the dinner dishes in the other room. I have put on an old record album to keep us company. I set up the bobbin to thread. I know the steps as I know the keyboard and controls of my typewriter: thoughtlessly and by feel. My hands understand the sequence they must follow. Everything is set up. My foot pressures the pedal and the Necchi motor revs up.

But nothing happens. The motor turns uselessly. The bobbin refuses to spin. I undo the entire set up and begin again. From left-side spindle, over the metal bracket, down to the bobbin . . . I carefully wrap the yellow thread a second time. My foot pressures the pedal and the Necchi motor revs up. But nothing happens. The motor turns uselessly. The bobbin refuses to spin. I repeat this process several times, first calmly, thinking that I must be forgetting a step, and that through the act of manual repetition my hands will remember the pattern. But no matter what I do, it won't work. The motor turns uselessly. The bobbin refuses to spin. The record continues to spin the maudlin songs of youth. My repetitions become manic. I frantically push the bobbin from setting one to setting two. Finally, I begin to cry. Not tears but sobs. I am choking. I cannot remember the motions and there is no one left to show me. The knowledge is lost, the memory gone, the Necchi locked in a past to which I have no access. My trifocal glasses are smeared. The bobbin will not spin.

Though we are not surprised, when reading novels, to find descriptions of what the characters are wearing, we are less accustomed to seeing clothes described in poems. There are exceptions, of course. Usually, when clothes show up in love poems, they are being removed. Wyatt's "When her loose gown from her shoulders did fall" or Herrick's "Upon Julia's Clothes," in which the "liquefaction" of glittering garments reveal the "brave vibration" of the lover's body. Or the moment in Keats's "Eve of St. Agnes" when Madeline "Loosens her fragrant boddice" and "by degrees / Her rich attire creeps rustling to her knees."

These instances are bound up with femininity and the trappings of gender performance. But what of clothes that aren't simply foreplay or a prop to be removed? Clothes that define us.

I've always been struck by the moment in Ted Berrigan's "Red Shift" when, about halfway through the poem, he lists three people, a boy, a girl, and a painter. Though we get a feel for all three, the only item of clothing mentioned belongs to the boy:

> Not that practically a boy, serious in corduroy car coat
>> eyes penetrating the winter twilight at 6th
> & Bowery in 1961.

I am surprised upon rereading to discover that the color of the coat is not mentioned, because in my mind I have always imagined it as brown. But why? Because it is winter, or brown is a boyish color? In addition to the lovely alliterative run of "corduroy car coat," Berrigan creates a slick internal rhyme between "boy" and "corduroy" (a word which, serendipitously, includes a boy's name, enforcing the "boyness" of this character). Through the mention of this coat, a car also comes into the poem, though the boy is standing on a street corner. I imagine that, were he to get into a car, it would be a 1961 model, perhaps a Chevy Impala, with bank seats, wing tips, and an automatic-shift wand behind a steering wheel. In other words, the item of clothing not only gives us insight into who this boy is—casual, perhaps not dressed warmly enough for the season—it also evokes an entire era, an era for which "Red Shift" is an elegy.

WAITING FOR THE
OTHER SHOE

Sometimes we come across an abandoned item of clothing in an odd place. It disturbs. On the one hand it seems unsanitary, we don't want to pick it up. On the other, it can provoke dark speculation. Three examples from my own life: crumpled among the decaying leaves lining the retaining wall, a child's panties, white with pink rosebuds; on the shoulder of the interstate, a single brown wingtip, old, bent; in the crawl space of the rental property, blue satin pants with black polka dots, one cigarette burn. What are the stories behind these things? Why were the panties removed? The shoe cast out? The pants thrown under the house?

Under the bright lights of a department store, we rifle through racks of clothes—all potentially transformative. The context and the fact that they are "new" shred any connection to the conditions of their production. Such clothes come to us without a history. But with abandoned clothes it is different. Lying soiled against odd backdrops, out of closets, out of doors, they call to mind the bodies they are missing from. They are emotionally connected to someone who is no longer there. Clothes given to thrift stores, or for purchase in a yard sale, are willingly surrendered. Lost clothes, mute and haphazard, seem always to bring to mind a scene of violation, separated from their wearers before the time for separation has come.

Jeffrey Robinson opens his wonderful book *The Walk* with some thoughts about the foot: "The foot is not quite a part of the rest of the body, not quite part of the mind and heart that direct actions and receive impressions. The foot is simply there, as the shoe that eventually may fit it is simply there."

The shoe, the foot, as "simply there"? Unthinkable! In my life, shoes and impassivity have never mingled, and feet, those wonderful appendages that make the wearing of shoes possible, are the bearers of glorious artifice and frivolous dreams. In shoes the construct and crumbling of the self, in their rejection, wild abandon, even anarchy.

To be fair, Robinson does go on to clarify that our feelings about the foot are never "simple," and that they tend to "exist in oppositions": "useful vs. the useless, the primitive or natural vs. the civilized, the animal vs. the spiritual," et cetera. These binaries easily fit the shoe as well. Though I might use slightly different terms: practical vs. frivolous, comfortable vs. cruel, plain vs. glittering red pumps that keep us safe from wicked witches . . .

Preoccupation with shoes can be a sign of strange psychology or power imbalance. Krafft-Ebing and Freud tell us of shoe fetishists, men who become sexually aroused when looking at shoes. In Luis Buñuel's film *The Phantom of Liberty,* there is a police captain who is almost comically obsessed with the shine on his shoes. The film cuts from the shoe of a sniper getting a shine to the shoe of the police captain. The captain, alone in his office, has crossed one leg over the other and is slowly gyrating his levitated foot in order to better admire the shine. Later, he reprimands an inferior for having less than perfectly polished shoes. His preoccupation with the mirror-like gleam on his official black police shoes has a whiff of the authoritarian about it. And indeed, hyper-shiny black boots have often been metonymic of fascism.

Shoes and civilization are wedded. For children, shoes are a stricture, a forced constraint on the wild animal body of the child. Since I grew up in a warm climate, I saw no need for them, and as soon as school let out for the summer, my friends and I began walking barefoot over the pebbles and cracks of alleyways, "toughening our feet up for the summer." It was a serious training. When I was about ten I lost my shoes on a family vacation. We were driving to Yosemite for Easter break and stopped off in Bakersfield to have a picnic lunch in a city park. Afterwards, my brothers and I piled back into our Volkswagen camper van "Lolly." It wasn't until we had almost reached the national park that my mother noticed that I was no longer wearing my brown Mary Jane's (the ones with the tiny snowdrop cutouts along the edges), and that they were nowhere to be found in the car. It was going to be cold in the mountains and I had no shoes. She was furious. But what choice did I have? In my post-lunch metamorphosis from human to animal my shoes had just naturally fallen off. Was I responsible? Those Mary Jane's had no magic in them. No shoes would until ... adolescence, sexual awareness, when shoes were no longer the parent's will forced over the animal foot, but suddenly became status, freedom, artifice, power, something that could lift me far above the degradation of my changing body.

In movies, magic shoes are always red. The eponymous demonic ballet slippers of *The Red Shoes,* those same that dance the poor heroine to her death, and the best shoes of all—Dorothy's ruby slippers from *The Wizard of Oz.* They keep Dorothy's identity safe from the wicked witch, the aging woman's hatred of the blossoming girl. Despite the vestiges of country life—scarecrows, lumberjacks, old shacks—Dorothy's journey is an urban one insofar as she has a well-kept sidewalk under her feet for nearly the entire time. She could never have walked over a real country road wearing those shoes. Whenever Dorothy looks down at them, the music swells with angelic sweetness, and she turns her ankle out that all might better admire the gloriousness of their sparkly red exterior.

Unlike most of the body (and for women, the genitals are included in this), feet, and therefore shoes, can be admired without the aid of a mirror. Little moments of shoe pleasure (like that of Buñuel's police chief) are exercises in gentle narcissism, reaffirmations of the self. When safely at home we cast our shoes off with abandon, there is no need for them because our identity is affirmed in every detail of the surroundings—all of our things. Out in the world (the dangerous Oz) one glance at our shoes reminds us of our purpose, strength, and inner magical stores. Bowing the head down while being upbraided or verbally abused may not, therefore, signal shame, but rather an act of defiance, of reaffirmation of the self against the abuses of the other.

Shoes can be stealthy. Or they can signal an approach

(squeaky tennis shoes, or the clack of a feminine heel down an empty corridor). No filmmaker exploits the sound of shoes more effectively than Robert Bresson. Whether over the stone floors of a medieval castle, or the cobblestones of a village street, we hear the clack of his characters' shoes long before and after we see them. Mouchette clomps awkwardly through her day in huge ugly ill-fitting clogs that seem both defiant, as she drags her feet, and restraining, as if an emblem of her oppressive situation, her poverty, and her obvious, indelicate sexuality. The night she gets caught in the storm, which ends with the loss of her virginity in a rape she seems almost to court, these clogs become so filled with water she has to remove them. Bresson's camera slowly watches as she holds up each clog and lets fall a torrent.

THINGS. THINGS. THINGS.

Helga Crane, the heroine of Nella Larsen's *Quicksand*, wakes up in a beautiful room after leaving Harlem and crossing the Altantic to Denmark: "It was pleasant to wake on that first afternoon . . . with that sensation of lavish contentment and well-being enjoyed only by impecunious sybarites waking in the houses of the rich."

"Impecunious sybarites." Those for whom luxury is not assured, and is therefore all the more delicious when secured. Helga's desire always to find herself, like the final touch, the pièce de résistance, in a tableaux vivant of exquisite taste, is the desire of an artist. She has neither the determination nor the wisdom to secure the funds—either through marriage or her own industriousness—needed to bring her vision to life: "Always she had wanted, not money, but the things which money could give, leisure, attention, beautiful surroundings. Things. Things. Things." We do not doubt her aesthetic sensibility—mostly made manifest through gorgeous clothes—

or ever suspect it gaudy or cheap. Larsen's prose, as elegant as the fabrics Helga drapes over her "skin like yellow satin," and the fine shoes into which she slips her "biscuit-coloured feet," leaves no room for ambiguity. Helga has a gift for beauty, and for that we excuse her selfishness, her restless questing after the impossible: to feel a part of something, and yet be held exemplary; to separate out purposefully, only to play the exile. The tragedy (or triumph) of the Romantic artist.

The Romantic artist is a contradiction produced by the social conditions of industrialized capitalism, the artist who, as Raymond Williams points out, cannot reconcile the vulgar Public that "noisily identifies itself" with the idealized "'embodied spirit . . . of the People'" (Wordsworth).

Helga Crane is a social creature, and a social contradiction: born in America of a West-Indian father and a Danish mother; from the North, but working in the South (when first we find her); allergic to "race men" and "race women" and yet violently opposed to miscegenation; of "fine stock" and yet "raised in a Chicago slum"; against bringing more black children into the world—"More black folk to suffer indignities. More dark bodies for mobs to lynch"—and yet ending up doing nothing but: "hardly had she ... become able to walk again without pain ... when she began to have her fifth child."

The contradictions Helga embodies come to a crisis one night in Harlem. Having gone with her bourgeois friends to an underground cabaret, she becomes swept up in the "reek of flesh, smoke, and alcohol," the "thumping of unseen tomtoms." But then she violently recoils. Her brief intoxication and association with the "vulgar public" proves too much. "[A] shameful certainty that not only had she been in the jungle, but that she had enjoyed it . . ." makes her "cloak herself in a faint disgust." Helga flees to Denmark, breathing a sigh of relief on the deck of the ship to find herself once again, "belonging to herself alone and not to a race." It takes two years in Denmark for that "vulgar public" to calm itself back into "the People, philosophically characterized." A people Helga begins to feel lost without. The "irresistible ties of race . . . dragged at her own heart." "I'm homesick," Helga tells her Danish friends, "not for America, but for Negroes."

While in Denmark Helga's artistic expression, the control of her wardrobe and self-presentation, is denied her. Her aunt dresses her up in exotic clothing and long dangling earrings. At first Helga is resentful, "she had a deep faith in the perfection of her own taste, and no mind to be bedecked in flaunting flashy things." But she soon gives in, unable to resist the allure of so many new things bought especially for her. It is a mistake, for by relinquishing her artistic expression Helga loses her agency. She becomes passive, turned from artist to model. She is painted by the celebrated portraitist Axel Olsen. The painting is a hated thing. This white male artist's vision undermines her cherished self-image, replacing her careful refinement with "some disgusting sensual creature with her features."

Without control over her means of artistic expression—over her clothes—Helga is made in an image she detests. In America her clothes externalize the internal voice she can't raise. They speak for her. At Naxos, a place of drab conformity, her "dark purples, royal blues, rich greens, deep reds, in soft, luxurious woolens, or heavy, clinging silks" assert her belief in "individuality and beauty." In Chicago, out of work and heading toward indigence, she buys a little tapestry purse with her few last dollars, an act of aesthetic defiance against the "smallness of her commercial value." Having decided to run away to Copenhagen, where she convinces herself there are "no Negroes, no problems, no prejudice," she dons the dress of fantasy for one last night on the town: a "cobwebby black net touched with orange ... bought ... in a fit of extravagance." And what could be more wonderfully extravagant than an artist's attempt to rise above the social contradictions that made her?

RED PICKLE DISH

In Edith Wharton's *Ethan Frome*, the doomed love affair between Ethan and his wife's cousin Mattie culminates, and then shatters, over a pickle dish made of "gay red glass." The dish, a prized possession of Ethan's miserable hypochondriac wife Zenobia, is stored on a high shelf in a china closet. A wedding gift, it has never been and never will be used, "so's 't shouldn't get broke."

When Zenobia goes on a trip, Mattie, hoping to make things nice for Ethan, sets a beautiful table, with "fresh doughnuts, stewed blueberries and his favorite pickles in a dish of gay red glass." During their stealth dinner, the cat jumps on the table and makes for the milk. Ethan and Mattie meet hands on the jug handle, and imprudently keep the touch a little longer than necessary. The cat, backtracking, knocks the pickle dish to the floor. It breaks into unmendable pieces.

This innocent accident reveals much. Ethan isn't upset, for he has no idea how important this dish is to his wife. Mattie, fully aware of the gravity of the event, fears Zeena's anger, and the possibility that because of it she will be sent away, separated from Ethan. They return the dish, shards neatly arranged to approximate its original shape, to its top-shelf purgatory, hoping its status as "disused item" will save them. Of course it does not.

Zeena discovers the betrayal. "Her lips twitching with anger, a flush of excitement on her sallow face," as she solemnly carries the fragments in her palms to Ethan and Mattie. Barely repressing her sobs, a put-upon Zeena demands a confession. The truth comes out, confirming Mattie's essential evilness. In Zeena's eyes Mattie has taken from her "the one I cared for most of all." Not Ethan—the gay red pickle dish.

In George Eliot's *The Mill on the Floss*, wedding china likewise serves as a symbol of a woman's things *apart* from those of her husband (though acquired through her marriage). When Bessy Tulliver's husband is financially ruined, it is the thought of selling off her "silver and chany" that most aggrieves her, especially her silver teapot and sugar tongs. Should strangers, who know nothing of their value, buy them, they are certain to be mistreated and scratched.

Her heartbreak over the lost wedding china stands in for the larger failure—of a business, of a marriage, of a life. It is as if the dishes are the only thing standing between these women characters and the suffocating truth of how great a compromise marriage has asked of them. They cannot work to earn back such things, and their one bargaining chip—maidenhood—has long ago been cashed in. They have nothing else to barter. When the things go, the sacrifice made to acquire them seems for naught.

Perhaps this is an exaggeration, and at least in Zenobia's case only the noblest of souls could possibly feel sorry for her. But there is still something to it. Even today, when many women can afford to buy their own dishes, a substantial portion of fantasy goes into the purchasing of wedding china, evidenced by the fact that as often as not it ill fits a couple's lifestyle by being, like formal dining rooms, overly elegant and rarely used.

Pickle dishes, teapots, sugar tongs. These specialized pieces evoke more than particular comestibles. They evoke the ideals of an old-fashioned middle-class home. Sugar tongs imply sugar cubes, a dainty item. Pickle dishes imply that pickles were once a fine accompaniment to a meal, and remind us of the importance of "putting up" preserved food. After all, how many times a year does one need to serve pickles in order to justify having a special dish for them? These things, like the words "respectability" and "ritual," have a quaint, outdated feel.

My Aunt Iris, in her late nineties, calls to tell me she is sending me some heirloom china. "Nut dishes," she says. What arrive are six little china cup-like things, two by two-and-a-half inches wide, three quarters of an inch tall. They are white on the outside, pale pink inside. Each could hold, at the most, a very small portion of nuts. "The only amount of nuts anyone should ever eat," says S. But I wonder, were appetites so dainty one hundred years ago? Or perhaps these are not "nut cups" after all, but had some other, now long-forgotten purpose. Seeing the undersea motif that decorates their perimeters—coral climbing over scallop shells—I think, "I've got it": a spoonful or two of tartar, served elegantly alongside some flaky white fish.

THE REPLACEMENTS

S. and I are getting settled in Maine. After a year and a half of living out of suitcases in Paris, our new life of rural homeownership feels awkward and unfamiliar. Our graduate-school-era possessions have been retrieved from their long airless sojourn in a metal storage unit and are unpacked into a new, much larger space. It swallows them. Though the house is old and in need of repair, it yet manages to make our things seem inadequate. It bespeaks permanence and demands improvement. It turns the things that had personalized our decaying rental unit in Providence into the generic trappings of graduate-student life. They look shabby and mishmash, as if their confinement had worn away what little value they had left. Some of them seem hardly to have merited storage, a fact that slowly dawns on me as I labor to free, with scissors and box-cutter, each meticulously wrapped object. My collection of spice racks made by junior-high kids in woodshop, which I had bought over the years at thrift stores and yard sales, are a case in point. I try to feel sentimental at their quaintness but can't. They look tacky and rickety. I should have thrown them away.

But I saved everything. It was as though I couldn't bear the thought of dismantling the one life with no image of the next, and viewed these carefully bubble-wrapped things as the fragile bridge between them. Of course, not everything I saved was a mistake. I am grateful for my old pots and pans. After cooking with a skeleton crew of cookware in a barebones kitchen in France, I feel happy to rejoin my mismatched collection. Some came from my mother's kitchen (cast-iron skillet, Mexican casserole dish, old handheld wire-mesh strainer, dented), some from thrift stores (two slightly stained but efficient heavy Dutch enamel pots with wooden handles), some had been gifts (Calphalon fry pan). Though no two pieces match, each records the memory of a specific dish. "Fireman's Casserole"—a dish my mom made from cut-up corn tortillas, ground beef, cream of mushroom soup, and mounds of cheese—belongs to the Mexican casserole. I cannot see the Calphalon skillet without thinking of "Superman Pasta"—Christopher Reeves' recipe for primavera (with an egg and Tabasco), which I took from San Diego's *Old Globe Theatre Cookbook*. Holding the wire-mesh strainer, I can see my mom scraping a spoon through flour in order to sift it. She is making my birthday cake, angel food with chocolate-coffee frosting. The Dutch enamels will always be associated with G., my good friend and cooking mentor, melting bar after bar of chocolate for the truffles we decided to make one year as Christmas gifts. The past pleasures of my eating life have been, it seems, as eccentric and varied as my cookware, from which I now suds off the cardboard dust and take care to arrange in my new kitchen cabinets.

A few months after we move in, my older brother comes to visit. Getting a glimpse into my kitchen cabinets he is aghast. How can you cook with such junk? He finds my old Teflon fry pan with several gashes in its nonstick surface and I am further reprimanded. "This is unhealthy, you should throw away pans when they become damaged like this." My brother has money and impeccable taste. He lives in San Francisco.

For my next birthday my brother sends me a beautiful set of All-Clad pots and pans. They are shiny and silver and heavy and grand. He includes special cleaning products with the gift, a paste for the outside of the pans, and a powder for the inside. "To keep them looking like new." A generous gift. I feel excited to see what kind of cook I can become with these fabulous pots at my bidding. But

I hesitate. What will I do with my old cookware? And then it dawns on me. The transition must be total. I cannot have both.

I grab the stepladder and begin to take down my old pots, not to set them on the stove, apply heat, and swirl butter in their confines, but to retire them from service for good. As I set the Belgium enamel in a cardboard box I realize that its interior may be too stained and its wooden handle too damaged to justify sending it back to the thrift-store existence from which it was originally rescued. The same goes for many of the others. Suddenly, the cookware I had been happily using for several years *does* look like junk, just as my brother said. Yet I feel melancholy at its loss, as if part of my life is being boxed and sent away along with it.

*

S. and I are visiting friends, an older couple, both writers, she known for her continental cooking, he for his scrambled eggs. We wake before our hosts and sit at their kitchen table trying not to make too much noise. We have been left a note: "There's bread for toast and eggs in the fridge." Because I have eaten such delicious scrambled eggs in this house, I am craving them. I look through the various cabinets for a frying pan, with no success. S. says, "could that be it," pointing to a blackened object hanging from a hook by the window near the fridge. I pick it up. The inside, which I imagine once had a Teflon surface, has been worn several layers deep and is now a scratched pale grey. The outside has become a sort of charcoal museum, with layer upon layer of encrusted blackness built up on its surface. The handle, made of plastic, is loose at the joint and wobbles. "No," I say, "this can't be the pan they use." "I'm telling you, I think that's it," S. says. Disbelieving, I hang the pan back up on its windowsill hook and opt for toast. There is a ginger marmalade on the windowsill that looks especially tasty . . .

An hour or so later our hosts wake up. Eggs anyone? We are all hungry for them. S. and I, worried, watch for what will happen next. K. walks over to the windowsill and takes down the devilish pan. Lighting a vigorous flame beneath it, he drops a good three tablespoons of butter onto its ancient surface. The butter skids and foams. S. and I share a glance of astonishment. But when the magical food appears before us the pan as object is forgotten. All that matters are these delicious heaps of yellowy eggs, perfectly soft and salted.

Put aside culinary things for the moment to think about the commodity. It is, according to its master definer, "a thing which transcends sensuousness." Not just a useful thing to be bought and sold, the commodity has mysterious metaphysical qualities.

Use value does not explain this aura. We do not worship and create an entire social system around a thing because we find it *useful*. In fact, use may even reduce the fetish quality of some things (like a red pickle dish).

Marx: "Whence, then, arises the enigmatic character of the product of labor, as soon as it assumes the form of a commodity? Clearly from this form itself." In other words, when does a made thing become a fetish? The moment it becomes a commodity. Commodities are things that leave us behind, that erase the "human brain, nerves, muscles, and sense organs" that went into their making. Zombie-like, they replace social relations between men with relations between things. And thus men become the proxies of things, and things magical, because they have cast a spell over their makers.

The feudal system had no commodities. Men were not bound by things but by a rigid, transparent, social system. But things were still magic because of God's power over them, over all things. The religious veil removed by the Enlightenment rethreads itself in the factory and is once more drawn over things, which, regaining their lost aura, turn back into fetishes. How different Marx's veil from Mallarmé's! In the latter's tremble, the neglected aesthetic asserts its independence.

In his analysis of the commodity, Marx reawakens medieval mysticism in the heart of the Industrial Revolution (the very same vein that John Ruskin and the Pre-Raphealites will tap). Perhaps the secret of the commodity's fetish-like quality is nothing but this: a nostalgic desire in the bourgeois Romantic mind for social relations to be fixed once again (whether backwards to feudalism or forward to communism), that it might be free of both the anxiety of longing for things and the fear of losing them.

LA PEAU DE CHAGRIN

In Balzac's fantastic tale *La Peau de Chagrin* (translated as *The Wild-Ass's Skin,* which loses the double entendre in the French, as well as the concept of *chagrin*—sadness, grief, sorrow, regret, impossible to translate!), a young man, miserable and poor, comes under the spell of a fetish.

Raphaël wants to drown himself in the Seine, but he does not possess the courage to do it in daylight. Awaiting sundown, he wanders into a curiosity shop. There, the Mephistophelean shop owner, seeing a perfect victim, gives Raphaël the skin of an ass. A talisman that will grant all his desires. The catch is, of course, that for every wish granted, the skin, and by association Raphaël's lifespan, shrinks. Though supposedly committed to ending his life, this newly-found object revives him, and then drives him to madness.

In a quasi-Marxist Möbius strip, Balzac's protagonist obtains a fetish to grant him wealth (and therefore access

to commodities, themselves fetishes . . .), and the fulfill-
ment of his wish becomes a death sentence.

It is a Faustian story, and nineteenth-century Europe
was fairly obsessed with Faustian stories. In fact, in his
letters, Balzac expressed his desire that the *Peau de Chagrin* "represent our century, our life, our egoism . . ." Even
the incredulous hero, Raphaël, is struck by the weirdness
of being under the magical spell of an object in the middle of this "century of light, during which we've discovered that diamonds are nothing but carbon."

Much of Baudelaire—both the man and the poet—can
be traced back to Raphaël, who dies after violently at-
tacking his mistress and biting her breast. A strikingly
similar image is central to Baudelaire's poem "A celle qui
est trop gaie."

Is the endowing of physical things with magical powers the result of diabolical forces or commodity-based
capitalism? Or are they the same thing? They are, or at
least they appear to be so, in the second part of Goethe's
Faust. In this section of the play Faust, far gone in his
devilish pact, murders Baucus and Philemon, an aged
couple who live in the path of his development, which he
believes will benefit the common people and "open up

space for many millions." Marshall Berman, in *All that Is Solid Melts into Air*, explains: "It appears that the very process of development, even as it transforms a wasteland into a thriving physical and social space, recreates the wasteland inside the developer himself." The unchecked logic of "ameliorative" progress ends by killing compassion. The makers become the proxies of the things they make. As with Raphaël's talismanic skin, the desire to eliminate desire can only end in death.

Fetish: any object of special or unreasoning devotion, or of superstitious fear. From the Latin *facticius,* made by art, artificial, facetious. And yet many fetishes, like Balzac's skin, or W. W. Jacobs's monkey paw, are animal in origin. The "art" in these cases must come either from the human spirit that endows the object with magical powers, or from the fact that all fetishes are connected to the irrational. The Platonic view: poets "are not in their right mind when they make their beautiful songs, but they are like Corybants out of their wits dancing about."

For me fetishes and talismans have always been things not only removed from human labor (as is Marx's point), but from any *social* value whatsoever (use, exchange). Unlike the diabolical specimens found on the forgotten shelves of curiosity shops, and handed, like poisoned batons, from imprudent owner to imprudent owner, my fetishes are ostensibly valueless items whose special meaning remains a secret between me and the thing. This is the only way to keep them safe from the nefarious machinations of those who live to shatter the illusions of others.

I have never bought or sold a fetish. All have come to me by chance, either as found objects or as gifts (but never as a ceremonious or wrapped gift, such as a birthday or Christmas present). When they arrive as gifts, they do so out of the blue, usually from someone I know but a little. An acquaintance who, by this gesture, suddenly seems to see into the very heart of who I am. The giver and I, once the gift has been given, will never be close friends. Too much is known already, and there is an understanding, a knowledge that would be destroyed by the quotidian banalities of cultivating a new friendship (telling our "stories," planning cumbersome coffee dates).

The fetish is always something with little or no apparent value; that is until, having tucked it away in my purse, or slipped it into a pocket, its magic begins to work. I may not perceive this transformation for days or months to come, but, if it has taken place, the next time I find the object (cleaning out a winter coat pocket before summer storage, for example), it will feel as though I'm coming across a long lost friend, a small thing I cannot live without, and which, I then realize, has been with me, silently, all along. These objects (I talk as if there have been many, when in fact, there have been few and, at any given time, usually only one), do not *earn* their significance. They elicit undue affection with little or no history, and fix themselves with the power to protect for no rational reason. I have one now that, impulsively, I threw into a suitcase before flying. When unpacking at the end of my journey, I found it tucked away. Though I had forgotten about it, it was now the reason my trip went well, free of all harm.

My fetishes are tied to specific phases of my life. When they turn back into useless, meaningless things, I know my life has changed, and must drift until the next secret object protector comes along . . .

THE IDOL

The association of a strong attachment to material things with irrationality and primitivism is nowhere better illustrated than in *Moby Dick*. In a book much concerned with detailed descriptions of material conditions, the only character with a maniacal attachment to specific objects is the savage harpooner Queequeg. Who can forget Melville's dramatic introduction of Queequeg into the narrative? He returns late to his room at The Spouter-Inn and —while a petrified Ishmael, quaking beneath the counterpane of their soon-to-be-shared bed looks on—performs a mystifying heathen ritual of indeterminate religious significance. Had Queequeg dropped down by the side of the bed and performed prayers, immaterial and silent as the divinity, there would have been no cause for worry. But Queequeg has an idol—an object that, for all Ishmael knows, may be no simple representation *but the very substance of his living god.* Stressing the savagery and strangeness of Queequeg's small black idol, whom we later learn is named Yojo, Ishmael first thinks it a "three days' old Congo baby" preserved like a shrunken head. This gruesome impression is soon dispelled: "But seeing that it was not at all limber, and that it glistened a good deal like polished ebony, I concluded that it must be nothing but a wooden idol." Ishmael's "nothing but" calms him, assuaging his fears that such an object might actually conjure forces beyond the control of rational man. However, it is clear that Queequeg believes in this object's direct relationship to, or embodiment of, a god, by his deliberate and ritualized interactions with it. Ishmael describes them in some detail for us:

> First he takes about a double handful of shavings out of his grego pocket, and places them carefully before the idol; then laying a bit of ship biscuit on top and applying the flame from the lamp, he kindled the shavings into a sacrificial blaze. Presently, after many hasty snatches into the fire, and still hastier withdrawals of his fingers (whereby he seemed to be scorching them badly), he at last succeeded in drawing out the biscuit; then blowing off the heat and ashes a little, he made a polite offer of it to the little negro. But the little devil did not seem to fancy such dry sort of fare at all; he

never moved his lips. All these strange antics were ac-
companied by still stranger guttural noises from the
devotee, who seemed to be praying in a sing-song or
else singing some pagan psalmody or other, during
which his face twitched about in the most unnatural
manner. At last extinguishing the fire, he took the idol
up very unceremoniously, and bagged it again in his
grego pocket as carelessly as if he were a sportsman
bagging a dead woodcock.

There is both mockery and confusion in this description.
In Ishmael's eyes, the idol fails to respond to Queequeg's
offering because it does not move its lips, but this tacitur-
nity does not fluster the savage, nor does it lessen his religious resolve, any more than the dead calm of a Christian's bedside undermines his belief that an earnestly
muttered prayer for eternal salvation has been heard. In
Queequeg's ritual we see a grown man offering living
nourishment to an inanimate object, and the scene reminds us of girl child offering a bit of cookie to the empty
body of a doll. Emptiness, it seems, lacks access.

Yojo is much present in the book's early goings, and in
addition to sitting atop Queequeg's head all throughout
his "Ramadan"—as Ishmael calls the savage's strange

Nantucket fast—the little black god may be circuitously to blame for the two unlikely friends signing on to the crew of the ill-fated Pequod. For Yojo tells Queequeg that Ishmael, despite his status as whaling novice, must alone chose the ship on which they sail. Ishmael is none too happy with this plan of Yojo's, but cannot convince his devout friend otherwise: "all my remonstrances produced no effect upon Queequeg."

Though Queequeg's attachment to Yojo as an object of religious devotion is understandable, this idol is not the only material thing the savage protects. He always has his Tomahawk pipe and his harpoon about him as well, needing them as adjuncts to his flesh-and-blood person. Even after Mrs. Hussey, the Innkeeper of the Nantucket Try-Pots, confiscates Queequeg's harpoon, "[b]ecause it's dangerous," the cannibal secretly recovers it, so that when the whole house bursts in on him, fearful his fast has turned harmful, the harpoon is there, resting calmly by his bedside.

How different Queequeg's supposedly "childlike" attachment to things from Captain Ahab's maniacal attachment to one single idea! The contrasting philosophies—"savage" and "civilized"—are brought into special relief when Queequeg falls gravely ill with a fever after "the tattooed savage . . . crawl[ed] about amid . . . dampness and slime" in the ship's bowels looking for a slow leak. Face to face with death, Queequeg again expresses his essential being through a material desire: he wants a coffin. The ship's carpenter obliges. Upon the coffin's completion Queequeg demands the macabre box be brought to his bedside:

> He then called for his harpoon, had the wooden stock drawn from it, and then had the iron part placed in the coffin along with one of the paddles of his boat. All by his own request, also, biscuits were then ranged round the sides within: a flask of fresh water was placed at the head, and a small bag of woody earth scraped up in the hold at the foot; and a piece of sail-cloth being rolled up for a pillow, Queequeg now entreated to be lifted into his final bed, that he might make trial of its comforts, if any it had. He lay without moving a few minutes, then told one to go to his bag and bring out his little god, Yojo.

His possessions ranged around him, Queequeg has the coffin lid placed over him in order to test it for size and comfort. He decides this final bed suits him, after which, much calmed, he asks to be returned to his hammock. Soon after this scene, which counters the argument that death shall remove all material cares, Queequeg makes a miraculous recovery and no longer has need of his coffin. When the object is brought out later for another use, Ahab upon seeing it cries, "Oh! how immaterial are all materials! What things real are there, but imponderable thoughts?" A grand philosophical statement, worthy of Plato himself, and yet Queequeg's immaterial materials harm no one, while Ahab's "imponderable thoughts" bring destruction to his ship and death to all his men— save one. Ishmael survives—by grace of Queequeg's materialist mania—when his good friend's coffin serves him as the ship's only life-buoy.

QUINQUETTA

There are some writers who animate the inanimate as a way of estranging the world. There are others who do so in an effort to tap the same vein of socio-psychological undergrowth that folk tales and fables so deftly exploit. In this latter category Russell Edson comes to mind. When "things"—and animals, given their linguistic shortcomings, seem often included in this category—speak up in Edson's writing, they almost always do so to comic effect, and at the expense of our trust in the human character's stability of mind. There is no question of Edson *believing* that the inanimate and animal worlds are actually saying the things he puts into their "mouths." Such meta-gestures allow a writer to call attention to the world by turning what is a very natural childhood impulse into an absurdity.

Children animate the inanimate world as a matter of course, and decidedly *not* to comic effect, nor to mock their alienated humanity. Rather, children, not yet having acquired the language skills necessary to account adequately for their experience in words, pour the unspoken remainder into the inanimate world, which proves a willing repository for their imaginative excess.

No writer understands the vitality of this bond between the young mind and the dumb world as well as John Cowper Powys. Perhaps this is because, though he lived into his nineties, he never lost sight of it. In the *Autobiography* he is unapologetic about the persistence of his maniacal attachment to material objects. His walking stick, dubbed "Sacred," is a prime example. To name a thing so generic as a walking stick is the first step toward initiating it into the human-object bond that can eventually create, through a focused energy of feeling directed toward an object over a number of years, something *like* the magical animation of its fibers. It is a form of worship, and as in all worship, naming is key. This is why houses with names seem more alive than those with only addresses, unless the house numbers—originally chosen by sequential happenstance—defy their limited locating function and, forming a mysterious connection to the inhabitants (perhaps via long years of letter writers writing out *that address*, and feeling a certain pleasure as they do so), take on a life of their own: "9 Ridge Road," for example.

Sadly, the long, slow, and often painful transition from childhood to adulthood usually requires a readjustment to, nay, *rejection of*, the very inanimate world whose self-sacrificing symbiosis once helped us endure the gradual squelching of our natural feelings as "shades of the prison-house begin to close." After this ritual abandonment we must worship our favorite things in private, hiding them in a drawer or closet, where they passively keep vigil over our infant energies, hostage to their solemn duty. Powys captures the complex give and take of this transition in a short, seemingly insignificant episode of *Weymouth Sands.*

Daisy Lily, a girl of seventeen, has come to the Loder residence hoping to talk with her friend Ruth about Daisy's mother's upcoming marriage. Ruth, however, is out. She has taken her aged father out in his bath chair for his daily journey to the seashore. Ruth's older brother, Rodney Loder, a lonely man of thirty, opens the door to Daisy, whom he has known since she was the little girl spending her days in the company of Quinquetta, "a little china doll with a face like Marie Antoinette." This knowledge of her *pre*-adolescent preoccupations gives him an advantage over the girl, who now has a "sturdy yet soft figure" shown to advantage under her purple jersey and dark skirt. As they sit by the fire in his rooms, a warmth begins to grow between them, an attraction in part formed out of Daisy's deep sympathy for Rodney, which fulfills his longing to be understood as a complex and desperate soul. This unspoken bond comes about when Rodney leaves the room to fetch Daisy some milk and cake. During his absence she chances upon a note he'd written only moments before her arrival. The note reads: "Rodney Loder—at the end of his tether." This mysterious message gives Daisy an insight into her inter-locutor and provokes her to send silently a tender wave of adult sympathy his way. And it is just as she does this, creating a sweetly gentle yet pungently erotic connection between them, that Powys has Rodney, "in that particu-lar tone of a grown-up person addressing a child," ask Daisy: "How is Quinquetta?"

Feeling as if a bowl of ice has been thrown upon her overwarm body, the young woman impatiently responds, "Oh, all right!" and then, with the spell utterly broken, gets up to leave. Quinquetta has blown Daisy's cover.

Though one might assume that Rodney's *faux pas* would make Daisy curse Quinquetta's name, quite the opposite occurs. Once home she gulps downs her tea and then rushes up to her bedroom. She pulls a dusty wooden box from a top shelf: "Hurriedly she pushed back the lid of the box; and there lay the china doll Quinquetta! Quinquetta was about six inches tall when she stood up; but since Daisy had relinquished playing with her she seldom stood up; but on the contrary lay all day long . . . staring at the lid of the box with no less earnestness than she would have stared at the ceiling, or, if it had been possible, at the sky." Daisy takes Quinquetta out of her makeshift coffin, straightens her clothes, and sets her up on a pillow on the bed. Though she does not apologize to the doll, her pampering amounts to the same thing. "You *shall* stay out, Quinquetta," she assures the "the beautiful little image, or at any rate . . . that invisible eidolon of it which had usurped a living identity." Then Powys assures us: "There are things, we may suppose, that a grown-up girl's doll does not need to have put into words; and so we may assume there was a perfect reconciliation between them . . ."

Although Quinquetta was a liability when Daisy was playing the attractive guest ensconced in a young man's rooms, her presence there at all brings up an interesting question. Yes, naming her broke the spell, but perhaps it needed breaking. Perhaps Rodney Loder's inquiry after the doll's well-being, though out of keeping with the moment, was a way of honoring Daisy's created world as though *it actually existed.* And perhaps, in so doing, Rodney was also acknowledging that the invisible sympathy between himself and Daisy also existed, though it was no more palpable than Quinquetta's small hopes as they hit the lid of her tiny coffin and bounced back down into her wide blue eyes.

Powys asks: "At what point does the idol, the stone, the block of wood, the doll, gather to itself its living identity, and become—as its worshipper certainly feels it *does* become—something more than the inert substance which is all that reason sees in it?" But we might also wonder, after undergoing this astonishing metamorphosis, how many things, unlike the little Quinquetta, are *not*, once their human worshippers have abandoned them to attend to serious adult matters, retrieved from the top shelf, but instead are left behind, in a semi-animate state, lying in the shoebox coffins of many a dark and forgotten corner.

PIERROT

The imaginative energy of childhood clings even to toys that have been tossed aside. Despite Daisy's example, children-turned-adults can be thoughtless in the rejection of their former inanimate friends, who, though unflinchingly loyal, are now forced to submit mutely at the scene of their own disposal (the film *Toy Story* 3 captures this).

But can a childlike "eidolon" be acquired in adulthood? The scene: Warwick Mall, Rhode Island. There is something embarrassing about this mall. It is out of date (1970) and leases to out-of-date retailers. But then I see him. My Pierrot. He sits in the window of "Wicks 'n' Sticks," a retailer of candles and gifts with a slight tang of head shop. My Pierrot is six inches tall, with a delicate face, and a little red heart painted on his cheek in the position of a tear. Tiny porcelain hands and feet stick out from the puffy sleeves and legs of his sparkly green, pink, and gold costume. Best of all: he has a white feather collar interlaced with gold threads that fluffs out from under his chin. His fitted black cap is painted on. My Pierrot looks plaintive, sitting stiffly next to a bong and a skull-shaped candle. I leave him. It is December and we are moving to France in six weeks. Everything must be put in storage. This is not the time to acquire new things.

But I do not lose him. Christmas morning he is waiting for me under the tree. It must have taken some sangfroid for S. to patronize "Wicks 'n' Sticks," even for this single purchase. My Pierrot looks happy nestled in his tissue paper. I take him out and bend him into a sitting position. I place him on my vanity, next to my mother's glass jewelry box, the one with the ornate silver lid.

Pierrot's magic has everything to do with France; with my having spent a lonely year there at the age of eighteen as an au pair, and with the fact that I am planning to return, seventeen years later, at the age of thirty-five. But this time I won't be alone. Had I not been about to embark on this journey (scary because we have limited funds and no idea what we'll do upon return), I doubt my powers of animation would have settled on the small frame of my Pierrot. Behind his wide eyes I see the wistful look of Baptiste Deburau in *Les Enfants du Paradis*. I see myself, all those years ago, at a wonderful red-plush cinema near Versailles. I have only been in France for a few weeks. My French is poor and I understand little. Yet the images still captivate. Only a year earlier I had fallen in love with Carné's masterpiece (with subtitles!) at the Kensington Cinema in San Diego. I remember the drama aroused when, after intermission, the film stock broke and the images were replaced with scratchy black lines, the sound with a repetitive clicking. The loyal patrons of the full house let out a simultaneous cry. They were so caught up in the story they had forgotten about the mechanism . . .

Pierrot is sad hopes. He is the tension between success in art and failure in love. He is the ridiculous idea that one person, or one thing, holds the key to all your happiness. Mine comes with me to Paris.

For the longest time, whenever I read "I have eaten / the plums / that were in / the icebox," the image of opening a freezer compartment at the top of a refrigerator appeared in my mind. Isn't that where the ice is kept?

How hard those plums seemed! How strong the teeth of Doctor Williams!

REVOLUTIONARY

THRIFT STORE

Walter Benjamin tells us that the surrealists were the first to recognize the revolutionary potential of outmoded things: "in the first iron constructions, the first factory buildings, the earliest photos, the objects that have begun to be extinct, grand pianos, the dresses of five years ago . . ." He then seamlessly links this "revolutionary potential" to nihilism: "No one before . . . perceived how destitution—not only social but architectonic, the poverty of interiors, enslaved and enslaving objects—can be suddenly transformed into revolutionary nihilism." A negation of the negation. When an object in capitalism becomes outmoded, does its aura as fetish fade, allowing us to see the truth, to see things as they really are?

Lautréamont, the surrealist precursor *par excellence*, famously describes the beauty of a boy "as the chance meeting on a dissecting table of a sewing-machine and an umbrella." Manmade things become the operative metaphor for human beauty. The miraculous made things (commodities) increasingly excite our imagination: *a patient etherized* ... We fall asleep, under the influence of opiates, hypnotized by the beautiful city and the glittering things around us, moving from miraculous object to mysterious mind: it is at this historical moment that the unconscious is discovered, after which it immediately begins to dominate aesthetic theories.

The surrealists, whose claim to the unconscious as Muse trumps all others, use a clever political backstitch to thread the revolutionary energy of the object back to its origin. The progression moves as follows: worker → thing → commodity → fetish → obsolescence → unconscious → thing → revolution. A rudimentary map. Benjamin puts it more eloquently: "The trick by which this world of things is mastered—it is more proper to speak of a trick than a method—consists in the substitution of a political for a historical view of the past."

In the surrealist program, things move beyond metaphor to become the unconscious itself, of individuals, yes, but more interestingly, of the city: "At the center of this world of things stands the most dreamed-of of their objects, the city of Paris itself." But the city's "surrealist face" becomes truly visible in revolt (the Commune as surrealist coup *avant la lettre*?). It is as if a weight of human freedom, extracted from every working man and woman, is compressed and stored in the objects that are the fruits of their exploited labor. Once there, it sits, awaiting release, sometime in the revolutionary future. Baudelaire's "forest of symbols" becomes a "factory of symbols." Another way to make a fetish out of the commodity? But here the magic can only be accessed once the object loses its first luster, once it becomes outmoded, once no one wants it anymore. S., from the other room: "why do you think punks wore vintage . . ."

Another angle: what if the revolutionary potential of outmoded things has nothing to do with things at all, but is yet another metaphor, this time for outmoded workers, with nothing to do once their jobs have been liquidated but sit around and foment revolution . . . or make revolutionary music, as the case may be.

SHELL GAME

Longing to move letters from filmy abstraction to mineral fact, writers send words through their hands, they move chisel, reed, stylus, quill, brush, or pencil over the sensual surfaces of rock, papyrus, wax, parchment, silk, paper. The printing press and the typewriter, though mechanical devices, maintained the sensual connection of the writer's body to the physical page. Dynamos marking pristine surfaces, they gave thought a palpable footprint.

The metaphor has changed with the digital age. The body has been demoted. Unlike their mechanical predecessors, computers extend the mind. As geological time makes a mockery of our lifespan, so computers laugh at the writer's blind faith in the "mineral fact." Digitally stored texts are safe from degradation, they cannot be burned, fragmented, or lost. Or so we are told. The materialist doubts the truth of things that have not yet hit the page. This may be why I have never been entirely at ease with digital correspondence. I prefer to write letters on the typewriter or by hand: old methods to suit an old form of communication. Or perhaps my insistence on these retrograde modes is motivated by egotism. I want the full attention of my correspondents. I imagine them examining my handwriting, my choice of paper and stamp. They find somewhere comfortable to sit and then open the envelope and read my letter, just as they might an old book, away from search engines and digital distractions, sipping a refreshing beverage, maybe even sneaking a cigarette, aware of the body, in measured time.

The shell of a dead computer has none of the charm of an old typewriter. A disregard for the organic logic of Nature's friction looms about it. These grey boxes filled with secrets line institutional hallways. We walk by them with indifference, shirking thoughts of their plummeting value, of the conundrum their disposal creates, the worst of "first world" waste.

Even if we imagine that with a little skill we could re-animate them, and recover the data, coaxing the shell to speak its history, no one bothers to do so. They are permanently closed windows into another life. Can we imagine such indifference to a discarded box of photographs and handwritten journals? But those forms are vulnerable, easily accessible, and offer their mysteries willingly; they carry the melancholy trace of intention. They bespeak choices. No matter how many dreams, calculations, images, games, or communications the owner of a computer may have animated through its keyboard, once discarded the computer shell becomes strangely nonspecific. We recoil from it as from a corpse. Both are soulless resources we mine for working parts. We can dispose of neither on our own, but, after taking what we need, we must rely on paid professionals to remove them from our sight.

An old typewriter may be disused, but an old computer is dead. A chilly reminder of the temporary timeline afforded the human mind. At least we can take comfort in the knowledge that our shells, unlike those of our computers, are subject to Nature's frugality. They can feed the worms.

Writers often perform ceremonies before writing, little offerings in private offices made to placate the Muse. They make a fetish of certain pens, papers, and notebooks, and bedeck the surfaces of their desks with special objects, all carefully oriented. On mine six stones from Campobello, shaped by the Bay of Fundy, sit, looking like a micro quiescent Stonehenge removed from any stars.

A relatively new addition to the collection of objects I deem meaningful enough to house in my study, which is extremely small and already crammed with books and papers, these stones have yet to be incorporated into any private rite. And though I have no say as to whether they ever will be, I have kept them close because when selecting them on the shore (many of their brethren were tossed back) I told myself that *these particular stones* had a certain latent potential. Private ceremonies and rites, rooted in the irrational, spontaneously develop when needed, filling in gaps of generative meaning, those spaces of irretrievable nothingness through which our precarious life-illusions threaten to drain.

I have a rock that I found on a beach in Rhode Island—a beach with far less historical significance than the rocky shores of Campobello, but nevertheless a nice beach—that I call my "Jupiter rock." It is orangey and has a striated surface, just like my favorite planet. My Jupiter rock remains inert. It has never become part of a private rite. I do not feel, upon entering my study in the morning, tea in hand, that I need to pick up or acknowledge the Jupiter rock, or perform a benediction before it. And yet, whenever it does catch my eye from its windowsill home I feel drawn to it, and will, nine times out of ten, get up from my desk and move to pick it up. While its coolness pervades my palm I stare out the window. The title poem of my second book of poems, *The Sense Record*, came to shape punctuated by such quasi-pagan interludes. Through the palm the rock fed the mind, drawing the energy out of the ego and into the vicissitudes of memory, earthly and unearthly both.

I read, in Virginia Woolf's essay on Montaigne, that his two great "bugbears" were convention and ceremony. As he put it: "As for me ... I cut out all ceremony in my house. Someone takes offense: I can't help it. It is better for me to offend him once than myself every day; that would be perpetual slavery. What is the use of fleeing the servitude of courts if we drag some of it right home to our lair?" And this from a man who, with great ceremony, retreated from public service to a tower in order to live a contemplative and studious life, and from a writer who turned the simplest of human interactions and emotions into topics worthy of serious contemplation and literary treatment.

But then I wonder, what does Montaigne mean by "convention" and "ceremony"? Perhaps what he is talking about has nothing to do with my collection of rocks, rocks that I all alone believe portals to "things beyond my ken." Perhaps the private ritual has little in common with the public, and individually created circles of meaning are, like my micro-Stonehenge, but tiny nodes of resistance against the great ceremonies imposed by history, commerce, and social control.

Woolf on Montaigne: "The man who is aware of himself is henceforward independent; and he is never bored, and life is only too short, and he is steeped through and through with a profound yet temperate happiness. He alone lives, while other people, slaves of ceremony, let life slip past them in a kind of dream. Once conform, once do what other people do because they do it, and a lethargy steals over all the finer nerves and faculties of the soul. She becomes all outer show and inward emptiness; dull, callous, and indifferent." Suddenly I get it. "Ceremony" replaces thought. It tells you what to do so that you are freed from having to decide for yourself. Ceremonies, which I had believed were meant to *enhance* meaning, do just the opposite. Like Kant's "emergence from self-imposed immaturity," freedom from ceremonies and rites is freedom from the empty meaning imposed by conformist human society.

I feel a puzzle solved. I have always romanticized ceremony, and longed (I thought) not only to be a part of, but also to be *truly and spontaneously moved* by events such as graduations, church services, and weddings. And yet, despite this longing, the very few times I have found myself involved in them, I have felt nothing but a profound awkwardness. The feeling is one of playing a game with random and nonsensical rules. All significance escapes me. I have, it seems, been privileged—despite fantasies to the contrary—to lead an unceremonious life. Now perhaps I can finally be done with this vain desire to "participate" and peacefully return to my rocks . . .

FAVORITE THINGS

John Coltrane's instrumental version of the Rogers and Hammerstein song "My Favorite Things" from *The Sound of Music* allows us to hear the tune without the words, to conjure the idea of "favorite things" via a light and pleasing melody without actually having to make a list. It is a relief, because the lyrics that Hammerstein wrote for the song are schmaltzy and difficult to remember, participating as they do in the imagination of an Austria as fantastical and idealized as the eternally sunny Salzburg through whose charming streets the Von Trapp children dance and sing in the film version. Of course, when I was indoctrinated into the ideological juggernaut that Robert Wise unleashed on the world in 1965, the alluring artifice of such idyllic scenes only served to make the historical gravity of the Nazi subplot all the more convincing.

My first viewing was in Mazatlán, Mexico. My mother took my friend Beanie and me to a matinee in a large movie house with balconies and stadium seating. The atmosphere was populism rampant, people were shouting, children were running up and down aisles, relatives and neighbors were screaming back and forth across rows of broken and soiled seats. Once the film began, however, the audience calmed down considerably, stunned by the aerial view of a lush green Austrian landscape bejeweled with blue and white castles and mirror-calm lakes. I too was instantly calmed, pulled into a state of amazement, desire, dream.

Though the opening scenes of the mountains, the convent, and the "I Have Confidence" bus ride are provocative, the child viewer is not truly caught until the scene when Maria, having just entered the Von Trapp family employ, sings "My Favorite Things" with the children on her big comfy bed. Since all children feel oppressed by their parents' rules, Maria's playful pillow antics and defiant late-night singing after "strict bedtime" is wildly satisfying. Maria sides with the children against their father. When they are caught, Maria explains to the Captain that there are circumstances when rules may be safely broken, "during thunderstorms" for example. She wins a victory not only for the children but also for the rule of individual reason against random authoritarianism. She intuitively knows what the plot will later show us: that the unbending nature of all authoritarian systems is an affront to reason, and therefore a form of madness.

Maria defies authority by recognizing the needs and fears of her fellow creatures in defiance of house rules. She sings "My Favorite Things" in order to comfort and distract the children from their fear of the violent storm raging outside, a storm that will eventually turn into the real political threat that was the *Anschluss*, which will need much more than a song to block it out. Maria uses "things" as her comfort tool, not actual, tangible treats or toys—objects with which to bribe children—but the imagination of a group of cultural and natural things that do not belong to anyone. Through the song she gives the children something they already have: a cultural heritage, a gorgeous landscape, and the delights of their senses. It is a brilliant gift, especially in light of the fact that the Von Trapp family, though fabulously rich, seems singularly lacking in any comforts. Their home is like a stage set, eerily devoid of things. Its beautiful rooms are empty of furniture, trinkets, toys, or books.

For years when I listened to, and sometimes even sang along with, my record of the film soundtrack, I repeated

the words of "My Favorite Things" without actually conjuring an image of those things in my mind. The words
were meaningless pleasant sounds, like the riffs on "Do-
Re-Me" the children recombine into different patterns
while teaching themselves the notes. In truth, I had no
idea what most of Maria's "favorite things" actually were.
I knew what "whiskers on kittens" were, of course, and
may have chanced to see a raindrop on a rose, but "Bright
copper kettles and warm woolen mittens"? "Crisp apple
strudel"? "Schnitzel with noodles"? "Wild geese that fly
with the moon on their wings"? "Snowflakes that melt?"
"Silver-white winters"? I lived in Mazatlán and Southern
California. These wintry pleasures were completely unknown to me. Neither could I, brought up on burritos and
enchiladas, recognize the litany of tasty Austrian dishes.
Clearly, these were *Maria's* favorite things, not mine. Not
so for the negative things: dog bites and bee stings. These
were universal ills, especially in the lives of children.

Meditating on this now, I think: perhaps "My Favorite
Things" is about the way in which what we love not only
makes us who we are, but can protect us from giving in to
fear. Love defines us and makes us powerful, while the
things that hurt and cause fear deny us our individuality,

turning us into nameless victims, participants, numbers even, in the universal suffering of man. As Christianity knows so well, nothing *feels* more unique to the individual than suffering, and yet nothing is more universal. How much more difficult would it have been to build a faith on favorite things?

FURNITURE

While translating Jacqueline Risset's book *Sleep's Powers*, I balk at the following title: *Étrange meuble*. I know it means "strange furniture," but in the French "meuble" is singular, "meubles" plural. The only way to render the singularity of this furniture in English is to add the awkward "piece of" before it. Feeling rather pouty about the whole thing, I settle for "A Strange Piece of Furniture," which is cumbersome and seems to lack the moody ambiance of *Étrange meuble*.

So furniture, as a category, makes up a whole, but the objects that belong to it can only be partial. "A piece of" something implies partialness, as in a piece of cake, or a piece of the action. Perhaps our inability of have only one "furniture" in English is connected to the verb form. To be furnished implies a completeness, to be decked out, filled with all that is necessary. You cannot justifiably call an apartment with one couch and nothing else "furnished." This impossibility is in the etymology.

A sampling from Webster's New International: furniture: "state of being equipped, as in armor or mind; supplies, outfit, equipment; articles constituting an equipment, as the armor and accouterments of a knight, harness and caparison of a horse, curtains and coverlets of a bed, etc." The concept of singularity does not exist in these examples. A couch alone is *not* furniture, but only a piece of it, just as a knight would not don a hauberk and then claim himself well-furnished for battle.

When the word appears in contemporary guise, as the stuff we use to furnish a home, couches, yes, but also beds, tables, desks, chairs, and so on, the relevant aspect is detachment. None are fixed in place, all can be moved. Furniture is distinct from fixtures. When used in the archaic sense of the "furniture of one's mind," then, the word provides an antidote to the *idée fixe*.

We cannot hold furniture in our hands. We move among it, sit on it, allow it to cradle us. We abuse it, it is heavy and blocks our way, we need to work in tandem to move it, it robs us of our independence, and encourages us toward stasis.

Years ago, furniture shopping with S., we walk through huge warehouses filled with massive squishy velour couches. When sitting in them my feet don't touch the ground, I'm a child, afraid of sinking like a game piece in between the cushions. These couches imply people and houses of Brobdingnagian proportions. They have drink holders and foot rests, and their backs recline until almost flat. "Furniture to die in," S. says. Couch as coffin, comfort as death.

Is this what William Carlos Williams meant by his line from *Spring and All*, "In my life the furniture eats me"? The larger context tells a different story:

> In my life the furniture eats me
>
> > the chairs, the floor
> > the walls
> > which heard your sobs
> > drank up my emotion—
> > they which alone know everything
>
> and snitched on us in the morning—

The hospital furniture watches the doctor make love to a woman, a lively, transformative sex act that also seems vaguely cruel. The woman's sobs (of pleasure? of sadness?) soak through the walls, "breaking the hospital to pieces." Their passion animates inanimate things, and then they themselves become those things:

> Everything
> —windows, chairs
> obscenely drunk, spinning—
> white, blue, orange
> —hot with our passion
> . . . .
> your bed, I wrapped myself round you—
>
> I watched.
>
> You sobbed, you beat your pillow
> you tore your hair
> you dug your nails into your sides
>
> I was your nightgown
>   I   watched!

Woman as furniture, eating the doctor, furniture as woman, swallowing him up, furniture as snitch, betraying forbidden passion, the doctor himself as hospital bed, wrapped around the patient, holding her. "In my life the furniture eats me" moves from surrealist caprice to realist image, a Williams-esque realism of the imagination, which is painterly, cubist, full of motion, and material.

Spring and All is a relatively early work in Williams's oeuvre, written long before *Paterson*, and that revelatory formal moment in "The Descent" when his poetic line slowly begins to move down the page with a grade of wide, gentle, rhythmic steps. The triadic foot. The ecstatic exclamation from *Spring and All*, "I   watched!" is an early indicator. The long spaces before and after the poetic lines in Williams's late work allow lineation to dominate over line endings. The line break becomes a line continuation, the space around it a part of the composition. The furniture, as defined by the typesetter—small bits of metal placed between or around letters to provide the blank space—eats the poetic line, and in doing so changes it from a fixture to a fine moveable thing.

A SHUT BOOK

Objects in novels are sometimes used as passive props to indicate social class. They can also provide a stage set against which the characters may act their drama. Such scenes are hastily described only to be pushed aside: "They lived high up on the slopes of the Hollywood hills, in a ranch-style home complete with Early American maple, nautical brasswork and muslin curtains; just too cute for words. It looked as if it had been delivered, already equipped, from a store ... Most of the houses Jane and I visited were like that." This description of a very particular interior, from the opening paragraph of Christopher Isherwood's novel *The World in the Evening*, though slightly mocking in its tone, intrigues. The psychology of people who live in "generic" quarters, in a readymade stage set, could prove interesting.

But Isherwood wastes ink. Within a few pages his protagonist will depart this scene, and the social milieu associated with it, for good. We as readers will never return to this "too cute for words" house, and thus we shall never know *why* Isherwood bothered to be so specific in its description. Why not just write: "They lived high up on the slopes of the Hollywood hills" and leave it at that? As we read along we realize that Isherwood's wealthy male protagonist doesn't actually care about things, except insofar as they provide him a way to dismiss the people he knows. His dead wife's letters, therefore, allow him to know what she was thinking about him, but never once does he mention what kind of box the letters have been stored in, what kind of paper they are written on, whether they are typed or hand-written, or if they are stained with the favorite beverages of she who spent so many hours composing them. The letters are a transparent window, a convenient plot device used to bring another viewpoint into a narrative, which, it turns out, doesn't actually care about the woman who wrote these seemingly paperless letters at all, except insofar as the chimera of her existence can help the protagonist to further his obsession with himself. She, like the things that belonged to her, is an empty device with too little reality to block the progress of the still living.

Elizabeth Bowen's *The House in Paris*, by contrast, uses material things not to simplify or dismiss her human characters, but rather to complicate them. In this novel the border between the material and immaterial world dissolves. Things have feelings, and people's feelings become things that can prevent their progress as effectively as the solid wood of a locked door. In the novel's opening Henrietta, an eleven-year-old Brit, arrives in Paris for a one day stay-over before heading south by the evening train to visit with her grandmother. The "house in Paris" where she is to spend the day belongs to a family friend who has agreed to be her chaperone and show her the sights. It is a house in which the will of an obstinate and controlling invalid has managed to stop time. The history of emotional abuse that has led to this bizarre stasis is never explicitly revealed, but the things give it up. Henrietta's senses are immediately accosted by the message they send: "She felt the house was acting, nothing seemed to be natural; objects did not wait to be seen but came crowding in on her, each with what amounted to its aggressive cry."

That "cry" will destroy Henrietta's resolve to see the city; it will also destroy the hopes of another child, Leopold, aged nine, who soon arrives to join her in the still mustiness of the house's fussy timeless interior. Leopold's hopes, however, are much grander than Henrietta's. He believes that his mother, a woman he has never met, will come to this mysterious house and take him away with her to live.

After placing these two children in a sepulcher of the past—the house in Paris—Bowen takes us to another house, this one in Ireland, and begins to build the history that will lead to the "aggressive cry."

Karen, who will eventually give birth to Leopold, is still a young woman. She is quitting her Aunt's house in Ireland after an extended visit. She leaves with the knowledge that her Aunt, who is terminally ill, will soon be dead and the house dismantled. Unlike its Parisian counterpart, this house will be released from its history. "The milk-glass Victorian lamps with violets painted on them, the harp with one string adrift standing behind the sofa and the worked Indian shawl for Aunt Violet's feet would no longer be themselves, once put apart from each other and gone to other houses: objects that cannot protest but seem likely to suffer fill one with useless pity."

Later, Karen, leaving a tryst with her lover aware that she has become pregnant with Leopold, herself becomes such an object. It is a metamorphosis without violence that she doesn't seem to mind:

Karen felt like a shut book, glad to sit back with an empty place beside her and let Sunday finish itself. It was true, to think of the chestnut, the churchyard wall, the Ram's Head door with its brass bar made her share the dumb sorrow of objects at being left. Like rain on the taxi windows, soft affections and melancholies blurred her mind; she saw inanimate things as being friendly to love.

Under Bowen's pen the failure of the human characters blends with the empathy of the object world to create a new sort of emotional physics, one in which objects bear the burden of the silences made by what the humans cannot bear to say.

TABLE TALK

As Elizabeth Bowen knew, few humans are able to perceive the profound empathy of the object world. To most, objects appear silent and dead. Mere furniture. Though all things, despite appearances and the limits of human perception, are by some definition alive.

Static objects are constantly shifting at the sub-atomic level. But we, with our vulgar senses, cannot perceive this flurry of activity. At least not in any way we can account for within the confines of our linear narratives. When it comes to the physical world, we miss most of what transpires, including the flux of our own possessions. We can no more record their gradual aging than we can our own decrepitude, which, however slow, seems to overtake us with a time-lapse shock. Things once new are suddenly old. Though they have never been still, our instruments are sluggish. The object world, patient in the face of our agitation, helps us to reconstruct the story. It absorbs, mitigates, and silently records the vicissitudes of human passion, subject to our limits, attentive to the scene. Devin Johnston's poem "Packing Up," from his book *Sources,* captures this delicate cohesion.

The central object of the poem is a piece of furniture. A "tea table" about which we learn neither the dimensions nor circumference:

> An Irish tea table
> someone took as spoils
>
> no longer speaks,
> inured to use.

These two brief couplets are filled with clues about this object and its history. We learn that "someone" took it "as spoils" from its country of origin. Suddenly we see a wave of Irish immigrants coming to the United States to escape the Great Famine. A tea table is a lovely object that conjures up images of afternoon entertaining. But is it a spoil? In such extreme historical circumstances, yes. It could have been stolen from a house of the dead, or, more likely, the table has taken on great value as an object belonging to the wealth of pre-famine, pre-immigration life. Perhaps the table belonged to a family whose fortunes changed for the worse. Whatever its story, it is a vestige of an era that won't be seen again.

The election of the table to the position of family heirloom is left in question by the poet's use of the anonymous "someone." "Someone" was the protagonist of the table's migratory journey, but whether this someone is a relative of the table's current owner remains unclear. Using the word "someone" also has the effect of shifting the focus away from the table's owners, past and present, and onto the object itself. We learn that the table, "inured to use," "no longer speaks." The human "someone" gets relegated to background, and the table itself takes on a kind of subjectivity. There is a willfulness ascribed to it. It "no longer speaks," which implies that once it did so. This line can be read metaphorically as well, to mean: the table is no longer valued by its current owner, in the sense of the commonplace phrase used when pronouncing aesthetic judgments, "it says nothing to me." Line four, however, changes the silence of the table from a human perception to an object reaction, the table is "inured to use." The word choice "inured"—to grow accustomed, especially to something negative—elicits our sympathy for it. The table's *raison d'être*, to be *useful,* has faded. And isn't it often the case that, while the use-value of new objects delights, that of an old one is taken for granted? The table, reduced from a spoil to a used thing, has been silenced.

Since the table is at a loss for words, the poem must shift perspective:

> Having crawled beneath
> to disconnect the phone,
>
> I constellate
> wormholes in deal,

The unusual circumstance of moving ("Packing Up") has changed the human-table relationship. Suddenly the human has dropped down beneath the table, "to disconnect the phone," and is observing it from an atypical perspective—more that of a child, though the sentiments that follow are hardly childlike. To find in this cramped space the cosmos-evocative verb "constellate" (to group), surprises us more than the grubby laborious "wormhole." And yet together they make a world, turning the tea table into a register of the micro- and macro-universe both. "Deal" is the wood (recalling another piece of poem furniture, Stevens's "dresser of deal / lacking the three glass knobs"), and with it we are moved back from the perception of the speaker to the pocked materiality of the object. This table, though once a spoil, has been eaten away with time. This image turns emblem and map of the fragility of human passion. The constellated wormholes become:

> black stars
> to guide us through
>
> whatever things
> we fought about,
>
> hooded forms
> of rage and grief.

Now we know that the speaker's sympathy with the table was born of his exile from the *other* human in the room: the lover who, in the wake of an argument, has become as silent as the furniture. By choosing the word "things," "whatever *things* / we fought about," the poet inserts the possibility that the intra-human alienation might have resulted from an argument over a material object (perhaps even this pocked Irish tea table) which one wanted to keep, the other to discard. With the lines "hooded forms / of rage and grief" this possibility takes a metaphorical turn, implying that rage over things is standing in for a more substantial network of complex emotions the couple cannot face. The table protects the silence and reflects the tension. It acts the partner in the speaker's exile from the human world. He is, after all, down on his hands and knees, under the table. He has lost his access to human comforts and looks to the table for guidance. The table translates the signs:

> From slipper foot
> to C-scroll,
>
> traffic of a dead world
> is testing a technique
>
> by which to make
> intentions clear:

The "slipper foot" (more silence) connects to an ornamental design in the tea table's wood (the punning "C-scroll"). The "traffic of a dead world" resonates with the ancient papyri called to mind by the homophonic "C-scroll," while recalling the immigrant scenario evoked at the opening of the poem. And then, the final turn: can this object, a vestige of the dead world, still record the intentions of the living? The poem's answer is definitive:

> you walk,
> and on the tabletop
>
> a glass of water
> trembles.

Unsurpassed is Thomas Hardy at capturing the quizzical soul's solitary bafflement at what moves other creatures, from the narrator's inability to feel the mysterious hope that moves the blast-beruffled thrush to "full-hearted" song in "The Darkling Thrush," to the "Impercipient" at church service, who tells us that he is "blind / To sights my brethren see," and that "He who breathes All's Well to these, / Breathes no All's Well to me." And this is exactly where Hardy begins his poem "Old Furniture," a haunting account of watching emanations of the long dead issue from "relics of householdry."

Cautious as always with his claims, Hardy's first stanza sets the scene:

> I know not how it may be with others
> > Who sit amid relics of householdry
> That date from the days of their mothers' mothers,
> > But well I know how it is with me ...

"How it is" with the narrator is rather unsettling, for he sees the "hands of generations"—all those who previously owned the furniture—still "dallying" with it, "In play on its knobs and indentations." There is no comfort of the sort that might be aroused were these visions of deceased loved ones, those sorts of wistful memories that can sometimes be conjured by fondling a special object that was once cared for by someone long dead. Rather, the identity of Hardy's specters remains unclear and densely layered: "Hands behind hands, growing paler and paler, / As in a mirror a candle-flame / Shows images of itself, each frailer . . ." We know not whether these images are the transparencies of lost spirits struggling to reproduce old patterns, or the energies of an oft-repeated human gesture trapped within the wood. All that is known is that each object in the unquiet room shimmers with ghostly afterimages of those for whom these things were once a daily chore or pleasure.

The narrator never sees a ghost whole, only disembodied parts. On the clock he sees a "foggy finger / Moving to set the minutes right," on the old viol:

> fingers are dancing—
> As whilom—just over the strings by the nut,

> The tip of a bow receding, advancing
> In airy quivers, as if it would cut
> The plaintive gut.

The mood of this musical scene is quickly dampened by the final apparition in the poem, a disconnected face hovering down by the tinder box:

> Glowing forth in fits from the dark,
> And fading again, as the linten cinder
> Kindles to red at the flinty spark,
> Or goes out stark.

The disturbing implications of this image create self-consciousness in the narrator, as if he is unable to bear the thought of the "linten cinder" that is his own life failing to kindle at the "flinty spark"—and going out stark. He brushes off the thought with a brisk "Well, well. It is best to be up and doing." This easy snap back to utilitarian strictures ill-suits a man who knows "not how it may be with others," and indeed, it emanates from the far less ghostly realm of contemporary mores, for "The world has no use for one to-day / Who eyes things thus—no aim pursuing!" According to the business-first rationality of the day, the narrator, sitting around having visions of the dead hovering over material objects, is as dated as these quasi-animate relics that "date from the days of [our] mother's mother." As though suddenly aware of his oddness, his solitary bafflement, he removes himself by ending the poem in the distanced voice of the third person: "He should not continue in this stay, / But sink away."

Hardy's things reanimate the souls of those that lived among, cared for, and used them, not those who made them. There is no revolutionary potential of compressed labor in the outmoded things of this pulsing household . . . unless that is, those who sit "no aim pursuing"—poets perhaps—might still be viewed as fomenters of forbidden thoughts. Such a reading might lend insight into Hardy's use of the word "sink" where we might expect to read "slink." Were it demanded that the narrator "slink away," we might think him a stealthy criminal fellow, hardly to be trusted. But the word is *sink,* which carries an old connotation of "to keep out of sight, ignore, to suppress." With this in mind, the voice that utters the "he should not" seems no longer internalized, but rather to come from outside, from those who would wish to "sink" the poet's vision of what will become of all of us, even those who are "up and doing."

Septimus is mad. We know this because Virginia Woolf allows us to hear his thoughts. As for his actions, they are described by his ever more frantic foreign-born wife, Lucrezia Warren Smith. Septimus's madness originates in a war wound, the loss of his ability to "feel." He learns of this deficiency just before the Armistice, when his commanding officer and friend Evans is killed. At the news, Septimus feels nothing. Now, in his civilian life, Evans returns as a ghost, the manifestation of Septimus's madness.

Despite his affliction, Septimus is exquisitely sensitive. Through his perceptions the material world—things, Nature—are enhanced, a real background against which he sees humans, both the living and the dead, as ghostlike emanations. Septimus sees the face of the dead Evans in a bush. No one doubts the bush. Dr. Holmes, whom Septimus calls "Human Nature," has told Rezia "to make her husband . . . take an interest in things outside of himself." No mention is made of an interest in others. Even his wife seems to come into his purview but intermittently, a failing she senses and which wounds her: "She could not sit beside him when he stared so and did not see her and made everything terrible . . ." Even his own body is apparitional: "There was his hand; there the dead." The contemplation of his own flesh conjures phantoms from reality: "White things were assembling behind the railings opposite. But he dared not look. Evans was behind the railings!" When Rezia, in an attempt to distract Septimus from his mad musings, points out a "troop of boys," it is as if their human qualities do not even register to him. "'Oh look,' she implored him. But what was there to look at? A few sheep. That was all."

In the final scene before Septimus's death, Rezia believes him to have come out of his madness and to have reconnected with her. She is mistaken. It is an object she holds in her hand, and not she, that attracts him. A hat and its possibilities. Septimus is lying on a sofa in the couple's sitting room with Rezia beside him sewing a hat. After "watching the watery gold glow and fade with the astonishing sensibility of some live creature on the roses, on the wall-paper," Septimus moves from his impressionist perception of the Victorian décor to a cubist game of dehumanization. Shading his eyes in various configurations, he turns his wife's face into a puzzle in an attempt to make it less frightening, in other words, less human.

He shaded his eyes so that he might see only a little of her face at a time, first the chin, then the nose, then the forehead, in case it were deformed .... But there was nothing terrible about it, he assured himself, looking a second time, a third time at her face, her hands, for what was frightening or disgusting in her as she sat there in broad daylight, sewing?

He is emboldened into facing his wife's reality by the "real things" around him. Rezia mentions that Mrs. Peters, the woman for whom she is making the hat, played their gramophone without permission. Septimus questions the veracity of her story. "Yes; she had told him about it . . . she had found Mrs. Peters playing the gramophone." In response to her assurances Septimus opens his eyes, "to see whether a gramophone was really there." What follows, though frightening, strangely grounds him, and brings him back, temporarily, to sanity, and to human interaction:

But real things—real things were too exciting. He must be cautious. He would not go mad. First he looked at the fashion papers on the lower shelf, then, gradually at the gramophone with the green trumpet. Nothing could be more exact. And so, gathering courage, he looked at the sideboard; the plate of bananas; the engraving of Queen Victoria and the Prince Consort; at the mantelpiece, with the jar of roses. None of these things moved. All were still; all were real.

From the "excitement" of these real things Septimus begins to confront his wife's face, and then, having calmed himself, he utters sensible words for the first time in days. Looking at the hat in her hands he says: "It's too small for Mrs. Peters." A light-hearted exchange follows during which the young couple poke fun at Mrs. Peters, "privately like married people," and Septimus offers Rezia advice on decorating the hat. He has an uncanny skill for seeing attractive combinations of flowers, felt, and ribbon. The completed hat stands in for a concrete accomplishment that, unlike the shuttling of his mind—away from and back toward sanity—can be easily measured: "It was wonderful. Never had he done anything which made him feel so proud. It was so real, it was so substantial, Mrs. Peter's hat."

After this moment of clarity Septimus flashes back intermittently into madness. Rezia leaves and he starts up "in terror." "What did he see? The plate of bananas on the sideboard. Nobody was there." He calls out for the ghosts of his emotional life, but is answered only by the material fact of the room: "'Evans!' he cried. There was no answer. A mouse had squeaked, or a curtain rustled. Those were the voices of the dead. The screen, the coal-scuttle, the sideboard remained to him. Let him, then, face the screen, the coal-scuttle and the sideboard . . ." Rezia returns. Perhaps hoping to preserve his momentary sanity through the resumption of normal, daily life, she resolves to keep the doctors from him. But Dr. Holmes, who "seemed to stand for something horrible to him," shows up unannounced and pushes Rezia aside to gain entrance into the room. Too late. Septimus, to avoid the approach of "Human Nature," joins his numbed ethereal mind to the material reality of the street below.

ESCHEWING THINGS

According to the rule of St. Benedict, monks should not own things. Not even the clothes on their backs. Monasteries can accumulate wealth, but not the monks housed there. Medieval people knew that beloved objects flatter the ego, which monastic life was designed to destroy. But did it? In the Middle Ages monks had an important social role to play as well as a community of the like minded. Even the ascetic anchorite or anchoress, though symbolically buried, had a busy social calendar. They were revered for their lives without things and many souls in need of guidance visited the tiny windows of their living "tombs." And they had God.

But what of those who live without things in the modern industrialized world? Daniel Miller's sociological study of a street in London, *The Comfort of Things,* makes the claim that the way we bond with objects is indicative of who we are and how we relate to others. That somehow our relationship to and care for things mirror our negotiation of the human community. In the chapter "Full," he describes a family of careful collectors. Christmas ornaments, stamps, clocks. They do not hoard indiscriminately, but rather study, select, and care for their things. Of the father of this happy clan of object-lovers he writes, "After watching him with stamps and with cars, one can observe how careful, patient and crafted is his care for people." The love of things does not stand in for the love of people, but enhances it. Against this portrait Miller places that of a ward of the state living in a completely empty flat. He had not, in seventy-five years, formed will enough to call any object or place his own. Moved from hostel to hostel his spaces remain spare and generic; he "had no independent capacity to place something decorative or ornamental within [them]." The reason? It isn't clear. But Miller speculates that his parents exercised total authority over him, an authority "that sucked out his core" and "the basis for any expression of his own will." Unlike medieval ascetics, this man had not chosen to lock himself away from the world. He simply had no capacity to bond with it, and therefore he could neither fall in love with "favorite things" nor meaningfully eschew them.

In reaction to modern materialism, some embrace asceticism as a political or moral gesture. They live without things by choice, as an example. They feel superior to those who remain dependent on things, and go ostentatiously "without." When I lived in France in my mid-thirties I had such an ascetic for a language tutor. Each Thursday I would take the long Métro ride from the fifteenth arrondissement to his anemic chamber in the eleventh. His two rooms were all but empty. A kitchen with nothing on the counters. A common room with only a poorly made table and two chairs. I would sit in one and undergo phoneme adjustments. Drill after drill on how to distinguish lingually between *Jean* and *Jeanne*, or *en* and *un*.

If my tutor had need of something, he would make it. Out of packing tape. His closet held little else. He could turn a sheet of paper into an envelope with it, or repair the leg on one of his rickety chairs. Should the subject of his asceticism arise, he would grow indignant that few followed his example. People don't need all of these things! And then he would share with me some of his packing tape creations and tell me how little they cost. He took pride in his ingenuity and self-imposed exile. Yet I couldn't help feeling that some psychological motivation lay beneath his rejection of objects. As if dependence on things meant dependence on people, an intolerable weakness, a lack of control . . .

Sometimes spartan living quarters are not a reflection of asceticism but of aesthetic refinement. I think of the cool beauty of the perfect rooms created by the neurotic heroine of the film *Interiors.* A few very fine things, each one arranged just so. The importance of the objects becomes so amplified that the people around them cannot relax. This was the case with a visual artist S. and I once met. His empathy for objects was such that he would only allow himself one drinking glass, one plate, and so on. Two glasses would create a conundrum. Each time he reached for one of them, he would have to justify his choice on aesthetic grounds. Why this one and not the other? What was the foundation for his choice? How would the rejected object feel, and so on.

This artist and my French tutor had one thing in common. Their relationship to objects did not allow for the provision of other human beings. Unlike their medieval counterparts, who eschewed things in order to cooperate with others, neither could be anything but an awkward host.